Baptists: The Passionate People

Baptists:
The Passionate People

C. Burtt Potter, Jr.

BROADMAN PRESS
Nashville, Tennessee

Library of Congress Catalog Card Number: 72–94400
Dewey Decimal Classification: 286
Printed in the United States of America

Dedicated to my wife,

Sara Leiby Potter

a loving companion, whose patience, encouragement and support continually uplift me and benefit others

CONTENTS

PREFACE

When Professor E. Y. Mullins disagreed with a colleague on a doctrinal point, he might give the reply he once gave in *The Baptist Message:* "If we do not agree on this subject, let us be brothers and agree to disagree. There are some Baptists who will not be a brother to any other Baptist unless he is a twin brother."

Baptists at their best, Baptists at the "center" of the denomination, have the sensitivity and humility to recognize that they are fallible. The diversity of Baptist viewpoints tend to complement one another. Those Baptists on the right have helped keep us emphasizing the basics. Those Baptists on the left have kept us alert to needs to which the gospel might be applied. The Baptist umbrella includes and needs us all. Great Baptist leaders, however, have been sensitive to and representative of the center of Baptist thought at any given time. They have aggressively and effectively followed the Master's instruction for making disciples and healing the hurts of a troubled humanity. The center may have fluctuated through the years, but the men who most vitally implemented our faith were found there.

Baptists are a passionate people! This book attempts to show why. No one is profoundly moved to service because of a sentiment or a noble idea alone, but because of a passion. Baptists have a passion for certain indispensable truths that make up or stem from the heart of their faith—a need for personal redemption; dependence upon God's Spirit; love for and obedience to the Bible; maintenance of vital biblical ethics; proclamation of imperative doctrinal principles; cultivation of an enabling fellowship in the church; relating one's faith in perspective to his culture; courage and willingness to exhibit an exemplary Christian witness. These things are the basics—and on these things Baptists agree!

I'm a passionate Baptist, because of the rich heritage I've received—a Baptist mother and grandmother who influenced my conversion; First Baptist Church, Corpus Christi which assisted in baptism and ordination; Baylor University's provision of a formal education; Southeastern Seminary's gift of theological training; a loving Baptist wife's selfless, Christlike life as a pattern for my ministry; a Baptist Home Mission Board base for nearly seven years of service in Philadelphia and Nebraska.

I deeply appreciate the total family effort in the preparation of this book. My attorney father, C. Burtt Potter, Sr., kindly offered his secretary's help in typing the manuscript. My wife and mother graciously provided "before and after" proofreading of the manuscript. My wonderful children, Christopher and Cara were real troopers when their father had to neglect them many evenings during the preparation of the book. The sympathetic encouragement of Nebraska Southern Baptists provided a great stimulation for the completion of the book.

A Passionate Concern for the Authority of the Bible

Baptists have an overwhelming passion for the Bible! They cherish the Bible! They always have done so. They have experienced the impact of God through the pages of Scripture. They have encountered drastic transformation in people and communities, because of God's work through the Book.

William Barclay portrayed the Bible's affect on Pitcairn Island. Following the mutiny on the "Bounty," nine mutineers, six native men, ten native women and a fifteen-year-old girl were put ashore on the island. Tragedy followed! One of the mutineers made a crude alcohol that killed everyone except Alexander Smith. Later Smith found a Bible. He became a new person. He determined to build up a state with the natives of Pitcairn Island that was based on the Bible. They would follow every biblical instruction.

When a ship from the United States arrived at the island twenty years later, the Americans found a completely Christian community. No jail existed, because there was no crime. No hospital was necessary, because there was no disease. There was no mental institution because there was no emotional distress. Every adult and older child could read. Human life and property was safer on Pitcairn Island than anywhere else in the world. God's power had brought a miracle through the empowering of God's Spirit. God cleanses and heals men and societies with the use of his Book.

What is there in life for which it is worth risking one's reputation and security? Several answers are evident—one's nation, one's family, one's faith, and the Bible! In recent years, as throughout Baptist history, men with passionate concern for the Bible have defended it with enthusiasm. Men with differing understandings of the Bible have

11

received severe attacks and ridicule for their beliefs.

W. A. Criswell was serving as president of the Southern Baptist Convention when he wrote a book expressing his sincere beliefs about the Bible. *Why I Preach that the Bible Is Literally True* found many challengers. In his next book, *Look Up, Brother,* Criswell went into detail to express the reasons he'd written the controversial book. He said: "I cannot help but write that way. I think in my deepest soul that there is a brand of liberalism that could destroy us." Some may disagree with what he wrote, but his sincerity and intentions are beyond reproach.

Ironically, a close friend of Criswell's with a divergent point of view on the Scriptures also suffered abusive reactions. William Hull, a dean and professor of Southern Baptist Seminary, preached a sermon in August, 1970, entitled, "Shall We Call the Bible Infallible?" The sermon later appeared in the December *Baptist Program,* and was the source of an avalanche of hostile mail. Here, another equally sincere Christian described his position in nonliteral terms, and was harassed.

Baptists hold the Bible in the highest esteem, even when they have differing ideas concerning its interpretation. Though Baptists don't agree on everything, there is a basic and indispensible core of convictions that Baptists vigorously defend.

Points of Baptist Compatibility on the Bible

First, Baptists insist on the competency of the individual under God to understand scriptural truth. Perhaps, it was E. Y. Mullins, the great Baptist scholar and statesman, who first put this biblical and historic Baptist conviction into words. Every Baptist who considers the personal accountability and access to God by a believer honors this principle.

On my way to a Baptist meeting in New York City, I sat by two nuns on the airplane. The flight from Omaha to Chicago takes an hour, so I had plenty of time to visit with my neighbors. When I introduced myself as a Baptist missionary, the nun seated beside me was curious about our beliefs.

I was excited about testing one of my theories on the basic difference between Baptists and Catholics with her. I said, "Baptists and Catholics both accept the authority of the Bible as the means of knowing God's will. The real distinction between us, however, is that Catholics have another authority in addition to the Bible—the church's interpretation of the Bible, whether you call it dogma or tradition."

The nun showed genuine surprise. She acknowledged that Catholics had two authorities. She challenged my assertion that Baptists had only one. She asked, "But who explains the Bible to the people?"

"The pastor and teachers," I answered.

"Well, there," she said, "there is your second authority—the people must accept the pastor and teacher's interpretation of the Bible."

"Not so," I replied. "Every Baptist interprets the Scripture privately before God. The central distinctive of the Baptist faith is the competence of the individual before God—the priesthood of every believer."

The nun listened intently, and then said, "Yes, but doesn't everyone interpret the Bible just as they've heard their pastor interpret it?"

That proved the nun knew little about Baptists. (I was reminded of some pastors I know who would like their people to accept every view they hold.) There was however, a morsel of accuracy in her evaluation. No private interpretations of the Bible can ignore the interpretations of Scripture that have endured for nearly two thousand years of Christian history.

The second principle that Baptists hold in common is dependence upon the Scriptures alone to reveal the truth of God's saving grace. "Scripture alone" has been an effective slogan for Baptists since their beginnings. Hull has put it: "The primary intent of our confessions is to insist that one may rely completely on the message of the Bible to lead men to God."

A third basic conviction of all Baptists is in the authority of the Bible in expressing the word of God. "The major cleavage in the Protestant church in America is no longer denominational, geographical, or even doctrinal. The line is drawn at the point of the authority of the Bible,"[1] writes a noted theologian. Baptists show strong consistency here. A

church historian records that Baptists "strived to follow the New
Testament as the sufficient guide in matters of faith and life . . . all
stress the centrality of the Scripture in matters of doctrine and
policy."[2] Clifton Allen expressed it similarly in *The Broadman Bible
Commentary:* "The authority of the written Word is found in the
authority of the living Word through the guidance of the Spirit. On
this basis the New Testament is to be accepted by Christians as the
authoritative guide for all matters of faith and practice."

*Fourth, Baptists would generally summarize the essence of the Bible
in a similar manner.* The basic truths to which Baptists hold would
be shared by other evangelical Christian groups: God redeems and
reveals himself; God selects his vessels, he judges all men; God creates
and re-creates, he rules as king and works in history; he is holy,
righteous, loving, purposeful; God is one in spirit.

Fifth, Baptists firmly believe the Bible is authentic. Baptist scholar
A. H. Strong said:

I would not pride myself that I believe so little, but rather that I
believe so much. Faith is God's measure of a man. Why should I
doubt that God spoke to the fathers through prophets? Why should
I think it incredible that God should raise the dead? The things that
are impossible with men are possible with God. When the Son of man
comes, shall he find faith on the earth? Let him at least find faith in
us who profess to be his followers.[3]

Clifton Allen wrote of his convictions on the Bible: "It is the
authentic account of the revelation of God in Jesus Christ for the
redemption of man."

Sixth, Baptists hold a common view concerning the Bible's nature.
Hull states that the reason for the earliest confessions of faith was to
"champion the Bible over any form of ecclesiastical authority by
insisting that it is the sole and sufficient rule of faith and order."

Southern Baptists adopted a vital "Baptist Faith and Message"
statement at the 1925 Convention. This statement was prepared under
the direction of E. Y. Mullins and remained intact for thirty-eight
years without alteration. The statement was revised in 1963 with

enough flexibility to allow most Southern Baptists to fit comfortably under the brim of its generous umbrella.

The "Baptist Faith and Message" provides the answers to five questions about the Bible: (1) *Who wrote the Bible?* "The Holy Bible was written by men divinely inspired and is the record of God's revelation of himself to man." (2) *What is the Bible's purpose?* "It is a perfect treasure of divine instruction. It has God for its author, salvation for its end." (3) *What is the basic content of the Bible?* "It has . . . truth, without any mixture of error, for it's matter." (4) *What main principles does the Bible present?* It offers three—the basis for God's judgment, for Christian union, and a standard of Christian measurement. "It reveals the principles by which God judges us, and therefore is, and will remain to the end of the world, the true center of Christian union, and the supreme standard by which all human conduct, creeds, and religious opinions should be tried." (5) *What determines how one interprets the Scripture?* "The criterion by which the Bible is to be interpreted is Jesus Christ."

Baptists agree with these principles, but they still have varying views on the Scriptures. Baptists seeking Christ as the criterion of their interpretation are more concerned about him, than statements of orthodoxy. Former Southwestern Seminary professor, W. T. Conner, wrote about the dilemma, "As always, my main problem seems to be that of being a good Christian and a good Baptist at the same time."[4] Conner commented on the dangers of orthodoxy, saying:

Dr. [B. H.] Carroll used to say that orthodoxy was making its last stand on Seminary Hill. Well, it looks now as if orthodoxy might have chosen a very poor place to make its last stand. . . .

They tell us that orthodoxy means straight thinking. The orthodoxy that I have seen all my life was rather no thinking at all. It was an attitude of mind that accepted traditional doctrines, and then in mind, lest it should depart from what was accepted, committed suicide. Orthodoxy is an opiate to administer to young minds to guarantee that they will always be kept under control. Mind is a dangerous thing when it gets loose. It starts all kinds of uncomfortable things. It interferes with the established order and . . . interests.

A valid test of biblical interpretation was offered by Strong,

Here is my test of orthodoxy: Do we pray to Jesus? Do we call upon the name of Christ . . . ? Is he our living Lord . . . ? Is he divine . . . God manifest in the flesh . . . ? What think ye of Christ? is still the critical question, and none are entitled to the name of Christian who, in the face of the evidence he has furnished us, cannot answer the question right.

Perhaps, the greatest problem about standards of orthodoxy that are arbitrarily set up is the terrible friction and hate that are created between Christian brothers.

The Wide, Wide Spectrum of Baptist Beliefs

Good, bad, or otherwise, labels are inevitable! Imagine a straight line drawn from one side of this page to the other. Let it represent the entire spectrum of theological beliefs within the Christian church.

On the far left are some extreme liberals, primarily found in non-evangelical denominations, who doubt the divinity of Jesus and the atoning work of God's salvation. They dismiss the divine inspiration of the Bible. They are preoccupied by social salvation and unconcerned over personal redemption. They dismiss miracles. Man's goodness, rather than his sin, is stressed. They abandon any concept of hell and teach that all will be saved. They are not evangelicals! Only a tiny percentage of Southern Baptists (if any) fit in this category.

On the extreme right are the ultrafundamentalists. A small minority of Southern Baptists are found in this position. The strongest voice for this view in the 1920's was J. Frank Norris of Texas. He finally left the Southern Baptist Convention. Most present advocates are not Southern Baptists. Many may be found, for example, in independent "Bible" churches. Exponents of this position characterize persons holding nonverbal interpretations of Scripture as being infidels or unbelievers.

Ultrafundamentalism came as a concerned response to extreme forms of biblical scholarship that denied the inspiration and validity of the Scriptures. A doctrine of an errorless Scripture became the fundamentalists' first line of defense. The central flaw among these extremists is the insistence that the only valid biblical interpretation is their view. The danger of this view is that having faith is too often equated with believing some orthodox doctrine, when faith really refers to the commitment of one's life to God, through Christ.

Adherents of this fringe group cling possessively to the 1611 translation, known as the King James Version. Many imply God has blessed only this version. Evidence offered for this contention is the testimony that every great spiritual awakening since the seventeenth century was preached from this translation. The 350-year duration is another indication to many that it is the only valid Bible.

Leaders of attacks against the Revised Standard Version in the early 1950's were among this group. For similar reasons copies of the *Today's English Version* were burned by extremists in the late 1960's.

R. C. Briggs, a Southeastern Seminary professor had an effective way to deal with opposition to the Revised Standard Version. One Wednesday evening he went to the church he pastored with copies of the Greek New Testament. After distributing the Bibles, he asked someone to read from the first chapter of John. The bewildered people replied, "We don't know Greek."

"All right," said the pastor, "if you can't read the New Testament in its original language, you're going to have to take somebody's word for what it says. Who are you going to believe—sixteenth-century Anglicans or twentieth-century evangelicals, including Baptists?" That night the congregation ordered more than two dozen copies of the Revised Standard Version.

Literal interpretations of the Scripture are compulsory to this extreme position. "If one began doubting any statement of the Bible, he had started down the slippery slope that, the fundamentalist believed, would lead to the denial of God."[5] In their legitimate reaction against the abuses of the Scripture, many extremists fell into a new legalism.

Here, then, are two extreme positions of so-called Christians. The bulk of Southern Baptists would be found elsewhere on the theological spectrum.

Southern Baptist Seminary professor Penrose St. Amant evaluates the variety of beliefs to be found among his denomination.

Actually, most Southern Baptists are committed to what they understand the Bible to teach. Within this spectrum of our common faith, we need to recognize the inevitably, indeed the desirability, of a certain diversity in life and thought. . . .

Nothing can be much worse than a dispute, theological or otherwise, where each of several factions seek divine approval for what it wants and brands others as liberals (who don't really believe the Bible) or conservatives (who have their heads in the sand) or moderates (who play both sides against the middle).[6]

A vertical line drawn at the exact center of the imaginary line across the page would represent the limits of evangelical thought among Christian thinkers of all persuasions. There is a need for new unbiased labels.

The large majority of Southern Baptists would be right of this line. However, there are two distinct positions—"right-of-center" Southern Baptists and "farther-right-of-center" Southern Baptists. Participants in both camps would be considered conservative and orthodox when compared with the mainstream of Christian thought. Both believe the Bible is inspired by God. Both believe in the need for a personal conversion experience with Jesus Christ.

"Near-Right-of-Center" and "Farther-Right-of-Center"

The tension between the "near-right-of-center" and "farther-right-of-center" Southern Baptists has been made prominent with the publication of several books. Ralph Elliott, professor of Midwestern Baptist Seminary, wrote a book in 1963, *The Message of Genesis*. Though nearly all Southern Baptists would have agreed with *most* of the book, it hit the book stores like a bombshell. The book was controversial because Elliott felt the first eleven chapters of Genesis were intended by the inspired biblical writers to be symbolic stories of deeper spiritual truths. Elliott's conviction that God used an evolutionary process to create the world caused a fierce reaction. "Farther-right-of-center" Christians felt the author had disregarded the Scripture, and was guilty of heresy.

W. A. Criswell's controversial book *Why I Preach that the Bible Is Literally True* brought protests from many Southern Baptist college and seminary professors. They feared that some would view it as an official Southern Baptist Convention position. Most of Criswell's book could be accepted by every Southern Baptist. The largest part of the book really dealt with "Why I preach that the Bible is inspired by God." This is not a point of contention among Baptists.

There were at least eight assertions that Criswell's book made that almost all Baptists would accept.

1. *The interpreter of the Bible must be led by the Holy Spirit.* Criswell's statement, "The Bible rightly read, read as a whole, read Christocentrically, read humbly and under the guidance of the Holy Spirit will lead us to life everlasting," is of universal agreement by Baptists. "The Holy Spirit . . . interprets the Word of God in Christ to all persons who desire to know the mind of Christ and to do the will of the Lord," is Allen's contention.

2. *Christ is the basis of the Bible's authority.* "The authority of the Scripture rests upon the deity of Christ," states Criswell. Allen wrote, "The Holy Scriptures have their essential character in their nature as the inspired revelation of God. Pointing to Christ and finding their meaning and unity in Christ, they are the Word of God." Strong said, "The authority of the Scripture rests upon the deity of Christ."

3. *The Bible is a book of faith.* Criswell's statement would be fully endorsed by nearly all Baptists,

Scriptures were not written to give us a course in math or in biology; nor were the Scriptures written to recount a full history of the chosen people of God, or to narrate a full biography of Jesus. God speaks to us through the Scripture, not in order to make us mathematicians or biologists or historians but in order to make us children of the Heavenly Father.

4. *Critics refuting the inspiration of the Bible are wrong.* Not much biblical criticism in Baptist circles denies the Bible's inspiration. Cris-

well speaks of the extremists who do, when he wrote: "The divine origin of the Scripture is now disputed in the name of scholarship, science and religion. This is being done by those who profess to be friends and champions of the Word of God."

Strong wrote similar words over half a century earlier, when he stated:

The universal presence of Christ, the Light that lighteth every man . . . gives me confidence that the recent attacks upon the Christian faith will fail of their purpose. It becomes evident at last that not only the outworks are assaulted, but the very citadel itself. We are asked to give up all belief in special revelation.

Strong continued in suggesting specific areas when biblical truths have been watered down until they bear no resemblance to the scriptural revelation.

Jesus Christ, it is said, has come in the flesh precisely as each one of us has come, and he was before Abraham only in the sense that we were . . . and the new theology will be of use in enabling even ordinary believers to recognize soul-destroying heresy even under the mask of professed orthodoxy.

5. *The whole Bible is God's inspired word.* Criswell made this contention, saying, "If we accept the teaching of Jesus Christ, we must accept the whole Bible, for Jesus Christ has set his stamp of authority upon the entire Bible." Seminary professors would agree with this statement, for it leaves room for critical studies of the Scripture. Allen suggests: "From the beginning to the end, the Bible declares that God has revealed himself to man and that the Bible is itself a trustworthy account of this revelation."

6. *The regeneration of souls is achieved only by the Holy Spirit.* The Bible "is the instrument of the Holy Spirit wherewith God accomplishes in us the regeneration of our souls," Criswell stated. All evangelicals accept this.

7. *Science doesn't contradict a proper understanding of the Bible.* The Texas pastor wrote, "There is no contradiction in the Bible to

any fact of science." "Near-right-of-center" and "Farther-right-of-center" Baptists agree. However, each would have a different concept of the phrase "proper understanding of the Bible."

Criswell went on to say, "Difficulties in the Bible are generally scientific, historical or ethical. Scientific differences for the most part turn upon interpretation." He added, "There is not so much a difference between what the Bible says and what science says as between man's views of the Bible and man's views of so-called science. Both views may be wrong."

8. *God used the human mind and personality in inspiring the Bible.* Criswell's comment, "God used the human personality and the human mind to deliver his divine revelation," is strategic even to "Near-right-of center" Baptists.

Seminary professor Hull similarly contended,

I would insist that the Bible is far more miraculous if it conveys the ultimate truth of God by means of ordinary men. It is relatively easy to imagine how God could transmit his truth if he somehow suspended all of the human limitations by which we live. How much harder it is to believe that he could disclose himself to men *without* doing so! This is the glorious scandal of the gospel. "We have this treasure in earthen vessels."

Interpretation of the Scriptures is the point where the basic distinction is found in the "Near-right-of-center" as opposed to the "Farther-right-of-center" Baptist. The former group maintains that the Scripture writers were inspired to convey spiritual truths behind the words that are used. Quite often they feel it necessary to use the tools of biblical scholarship to uncover that truth. The tools are "lower criticism" and "higher criticism." Lower criticism is a study of problems in the text and involves efforts to determine which of many manuscripts is the earliest and most reliable. Higher criticism refers to efforts to ascertain the author, date, and character of the book.

"Farther-right-of-center" Baptists embrace "lower criticism." They want the most accurate texts. They generally frown on the other critical pursuit. Criswell spoke of the validity and dangers, saying: "While an erudite and scholarly pursuit that is perfectly legitimate and vital, higher criticism is often turned into channels of blasphemy and defamation because of the presuppositions of the men who are thus studying the word of God." This group insist that the Bible was meant to be interpreted literally. This is the key point of departure between the two groups of Baptists.

The Criswell book could not be accepted in its entirety because of this basic difference. Three concepts of the Bible that were listed in the book would give difficulty to the "Near-right-of-center" Baptists.

First, they cannot accept the view that the Bible was meant to be interpreted literally. Duke McCall, president of Southern Baptist Seminary, has presented a cassette recording entitled, "Baptist Views of the Bible." He explains that some sincere Baptists feel every *word* was inspired in the Bible, and therefore they maintain a literal interpretation. Other sincere Baptists feel that the *writers* were inspired. These in the latter category use a critical study of the texts that,

assumes that both the writer and reader have human limitations. These limitations produce many problems for the interpreter; but they reflect the freedom with which God has endowed man as well as the dignity and responsibility entrusted to man. The role of the Christian is not so much that of a knower—one, who knows—as that of a learner or disciple. The biblical writers were uniquely inspired of the Holy Spirit. This message is not a message men might have stumbled upon, but rather the message wherein God reveals himself to men, making known his intention for his creation.

Criswell correctly assessed objections that many seminary professors would have to his views; "This is called the verbal theory of inspiration which is vehemently denied by many modern theologians. They say it is too mechanical. They say it degrades the writers to the level of machines."

Literalists resent the term "mechanical inspiration," saying it represents prejudice and error. Their critics are convinced it's an accurate portrayal, since the human element appears to be reduced to a passive transmitter of God's revelation.

Hull challenged the literal theory in his controversial sermon. He stated: "There are no infallible rules for translators . . . Even if we did have a perfect text rendered in a perfect translation, we would still be far from an infallible Bible because it would still have to be explained by fallible interpreters." Hull sought to portray the relationship of the Bible to Christ, stating, "There is deep wisdom in the recognition that the teaching of Christ determines the significance of the Bible rather than the meaning of the Bible determining the significance of Christ."

Hull warned of the dangers of being captive to the literal interpretation. He reminded his congregation of the Catholic system, which developed the Vulgate as the stabilized text of the church. They then refused to allow the version to be translated, even after Latin became a dead language. The teaching office of the Roman church became the infallible interpreter to an unchanging book.

Hull sees a parallel in the reluctance of some to give up the single King James translation. Clinging to the King James meant refusing to translate archaisms. The adoption of statements about the Bible, rather than trusting the Bible itself, Hull felt, was dangerous.

Second, "Near-right-of-center" Baptists couldn't agree with the contention that the Bible claims to be infallible.

There is a clear-cut difference of opinion at this item. Criswell wrote, "The most convincing of all the proofs and arguments for the verbal inspiration of the Bible is the fact that the Lord Jesus regarded it and treated it as such."

Hull replied with a meditating view, saying it would be "ironic to claim something for the Bible which it does not claim to itself." He contends the Bible is infallible in another sense.

Third, they cannot accept the contention that there is power inherent in the Scriptures themselves. Criswell stated, "This is one of the reasons why I believe that the Bible is literally true: namely because of the marvelous effect it has upon those who hear it and read it."

Strong's view was: "Nowhere are we told that the Scripture of itself

is able to convince the sinner or bring him to God. It is the glittering
sword but it is the sword of the Spirit and unless the Spirit uses it,
it will never pierce the heart."

The Baptist Search for Biblical Truth

All Baptists search for the truth of God that is revealed in the
Scriptures. Because they search in different ways, they sometimes
reach differing conclusions. "Farther-right-of-center" scholars often
maintain that, in Criswell's words, "On the original parchment every
sentence, word, line, mark, point, pen stroke, jot and tittle were put
there by inspiration of God."   They maintain that the closer they get
to the original manuscripts, the clearer is the truth of God.

"Near-to-the-right-of-center" theologian Strong gives an additional
point of view. He stated: "Neither evolution nor the higher criticism
has any terrors to one who regards them as parts of Christ's creating
and educational process. The Christ in whom are hid all the treasures
of wisdom and knowledge himself furnished all the needed safeguards
and limitations."

W. T. Conner would be considered a strong conservative by the
measuring rod of other Christian thinkers. However, the Southwestern Seminary theologian said:

I have not changed on my liberal point of view but have gradually
gotten over the newness of it all so that I feel a little more at home
therein. I think liberalism is more an atmosphere in which one lives
than a set of theological assumptions. A man can be liberal without
being a liberal and without being crassly vocal. . . .

The premillenialists around here have decided that I am a Christian
after all and the posts don't know what it is all about anyway.

The intangible test of orthodoxy must have been put to Conner on
numerous occasions. T. B. Maston says:

It will interfere with the search for truth when orthodoxy as such
is the final test of truth. How unfortunate if we accept a thing as true
simply because it is considered orthodox. Also, how tragic for us and
for the cause of truth if our question as we search for truth, is whether

or not it is orthodox. The supreme question should be, 'Is it true?'

Orthodoxy will also interfere with our search for truth if it erects artificial barriers for us in that search. The creative mind must be free from the fear of truth. The creative Christian mind is a disciplined mind working under the guiding impulse of the divine Spirit with a deep sense of its responsibility to mankind in general but to God in particular.

Could it be that Southern Baptists have not contributed their share of creative scholarship because they have been too much under the constraints of heresy hunters?[7]

Why do Christian men flare up when their views are challenged? Someone has suggested, "I defend something, not because it is true, but because I've said it was true." Perhaps, human pride explains the passionate, emotional explosions between fellow Baptists in some instances.

Criswell voiced another's quote to characterize many of his liberal critics, "I find that so-called liberals can be the most illiberal of men. They often degenerate into religious critics and censors. They indulge in flings at the orthodox and have little to say that is positive and constructive." Criswell continued with his own comment, "This is so true. I have, myself, felt the bitter sting of these unchristian castigations."

Not long after he'd written these remarks, Criswell, a champion of conservatism, felt the "bitter sting of unchristian castigations" at the 1970 Southern Baptist Convention by fundamentalist extremists. These critics felt Criswell favored the liberal views in his rulings on various resolutions at the Convention.

Scholarly fundamentalist E. John Carnell gave an appraisal of radical fundamentalists: "Fundamentalism is a paradoxical position. It sees the heresy in untruth but not in unloviness. If it has the most truth, it has the least grace, since it distrusts courtesy and diplomacy. Fundamentalism forgets that orthodox truth without orthodox love profits nothing."[8]

What is the proper way for men with strong conflicting opinions to coexist? An ideal example of dealing with divergent theological views was illustrated by two former Southern Baptist Convention presidents. In 1920 E. Y. Mullins, president of Southern Baptist Seminary, and J. B. Gambrell, editor of Texas' *Baptist Standard,* made a trip around the world together. They represented their denomination on a survey of war-devastated Europe. The two men were far apart on theological issues. When M. E. Dodd heard of the travel arrangements he commented that they had enough in common to be congenial and enough differences to make it interesting.

After the trip, Mullins said, "We discussed everything you can think of. We agreed on the great things. We did not always agree on other things."[9]

The other traveler, Dr. Gambrell, gave this evaluation,

Dr. Mullins and I discussed and settled nearly all of the questions which have divided Baptists into small factions, or to be more accurate, the questions which have developed factions within the denomination. Sometimes we settled them by disagreeing and letting it go at that. On some points I found him very difficult to convince and was compelled to let him have his own notions. I have about come to the conclusion that I will not live long enough to bring all the brethren to my views on the millenium, who wrote Hebrews, who was Cain's wife, and a whole brood of questions concerning men, methods, and historical incidents. I found President Mullins about as reasonable as most of our leaders, and a sight more so than a number of would-be leaders. I can say this for him, he agreed with me as often as I agreed with him. . . . By the closest fellowship with President Mullins for months, I feel that my own spiritual and intellectual life has been greatly and permanently enriched. He is a devout Christian without affectation.

Several ingredients are essential for Baptists with opposing views to behave as Christian brothers.

First, there must be an earnest effort to communicate. Hull described his intent to relate to those with differing points of opinion, at the conclusion of his sermon, "At the end I tried to reach out to the other side and say, 'At best I think you are trying to say the Bible is authoritative, that it's unique, that it does convey an infallible message.' I emphasized that which we can unite on is not some phrase about the Bible, but Christ."

Second, there must be an attitude of openness and toleration. Criswell illustrates this trait in his statement,

I do not quarrel with a man confessing he believes in these sources if he honestly accepts the Bible as the Word of God. Some of the dearest friends I have in the world, men who are more devout and dedicated to Christ than I, firmly believe in the Graf-Wellhausen-Kuenen approach to the makeup of the Old Testament. I do not believe a syllable of the conclusions of these German higher critics, but these good men do. If they believe the Bible to be the Word of God, even though they accept some of these higher critical conclusions, I have no word to say against them.

Third, love for one's brother grows out of one's love for Christ. Mullins described the tension early in the century:

The lines of doctrinal cleavage are as radical as at any time in the past, but the issues are new. As usual, the extreme parties are doing the most harm. On one side is the ultra-conservative, the man of the hammer and anvil method, who relies chiefly upon denunciation of opponents, and cannot tolerate discussion on a fraternal basis; and on the other is the ultra-progressive whose lofty contempt of the traditionalists shuts him out from the sane scholarship and wise leadership.[10]

The analysis Mullins submitted sounds strangely relevant for the 1970's. Likewise, Mullins' solution for the dilemma of more than half a century ago, is still applicable: "The really safe leaders of thought, however, are between the extremes. They have sympathy with those who are perplexed, but they are also resolved to be loyal to Christ and his Gospel." The competency of the soul before God is the watershed of Baptist doctrine, and the key to all that we are.

2 A Passionate Concern for Personal Redemption

That great Baptist giant, B. H. Carroll, was an avowed infidel or unbeliever until he was twenty-seven years of age. He'd been baptized as a thirteen-year-old boy, because he knew the answers to historical biblical questions. He neither felt nor believed he was saved! Fourteen years later his mother invited the unbelieving son to attend a revival meeting. He agreed to attend one last time. It was a poor sermon from an ineffective preacher. Carroll was challenged by the preacher's closing appeal. The minister looked over the congregation, saying, "You out there who scoff at Christianity, what do you have that's better?"

That question pierced the hardened facade that had protected Carroll. He knew that none of his own experimentations brought peace. Carroll realized that Christianity might be the answer after all. Moments later at the mourner's bench, the convicted unbeliever experienced personal redemption through Jesus Christ.

Alvin Toffler's *Future Shock* reports the unexpected contemporary passion for mystical experiences. The phenomenon of astrology buffs, yoga enthusiasts, and Zen Buddhist adherents has had a snowballing impact on the American public. Others conscientiously engage in witchcraft, seances, or Satan worship. The quest for the Judeo-Christian God has had unbelievable accelerating popularity.

Toffler suggests that the revival of the mystical is attributable to disillusionment with the scientific and rational elements in modern society. Most theologians and psychologists would accept this contention as a part of the answer. Man's captivity to evil and guilt over evil are obvious accompanying reasons. This prompted Oswald Chambers to stress the greatness of Christ's sacrificial action for man over any benefits man receives:

Never confuse the Cross of Christ with the benefits that flow from it. For all his doctrine Paul's one great passion was the Cross of Christ, not salvation, nor sanctification, but the great truth that God so loved the world that he gave His only begotten Son.[1]

William J. Wolfe in *No Cross, No Crown* described the four basic evils from which every man needs deliverance—suffering, error, sin, and death. These evils "are the ones from which salvation is sought in nearly every religion and philosophy of life."

Inwardly, every man recognizes the need for this salvation. Men differ widely on how they think the salvation can be achieved. Most of the world's religions teach a salvation that is attained by personal betterment. Men seek to achieve their deity's pleasure by sacrifice or progress toward perfection. Evangelical Christianity contends that the answer is found in the unique redemption God performed in Christ's death. Baptists are among the remnant that maintain Christ alone was qualified for this mission. Apart from this personal redemption there would be no Baptists. The Baptist contention is that Christ alone is perfect and man's best efforts can't keep pace with the spiraling infection of his own sin. Christ's death or passion becomes the Baptist passion. Only here does man escape the evils of suffering, error, sin, and death.

The Effect of Personal Redemption

I was making my first trip across Nebraska westward by plane. An attractive young career woman boarded the plane in Lincoln and sat beside me. She was on a business trip for the telephone company. When she discovered I was a minister, she spoke sentimentally of her upbringing in another Protestant denomination.

"The church is behind the times and no longer of much value," she exclaimed. "It should be busy helping to feed the poor, rather than just talking about God," she added.

I told her a story that had occurred within the past several months, verifying the relevance of the church. A group of committed Christian college students had assisted in an inner-city Southern Baptist church

in Philadelphia. They befriended Don, the watchman of a neighborhood laundrymat, who was quite lonely. The students discovered that
their new friend was an atheist, and had served eighteen years in
prison for murder.

The students took a genuine interest in him. They took him on trips
and transported him to the doctor's office when he was severely
sunburned. After ten weeks of transmitting the love of God through
expressions of concern, Don committed his life to Christ.

Today, I told my traveling companion, Don is attending college
to prepare for the ministry. He feels God's leadership to return to the
prisons as a chaplain. "If God can work through the church to change
an atheistic killer into an ambassador of love, does this make the
church seem relevant?" I asked her.

"Yes," she conceded. "If a killer can be changed to a lover, because
of Christ, I guess the church is still worthwhile."

The new life this convert experienced was the result of God's re-
moval of guilt and sin from his life. God's forgiveness was so overwhelming that he was changed into a different person. This is the
meaning of redemption to evangelical Christians.

Evidence of a Personal Redemption

Jesus intended for his followers to be different in their attitudes and
actions after they had trusted him. Certainly they were different in
their relationship to God with their sins forgiven. He expected his
redemptive work to be apparent to others. "By their fruits, ye shall
know them," he said. Critics of Jesus' early followers exclaimed,
"These that have turned the world upside down are come hither also"
(Acts 17:6).

C. S. Lewis, the late English Christian, suggested ways to recognize
Christians who are thoroughly immersed in Christlikeness.

Some . . . are still hardly recognisable: but others can be recognised. Every now and then one meets them. Their very voices and
faces are different from ours; stronger, quieter, happier, more radiant.
They begin where most of us leave off. They are, I say, recognisable;

but you must know what to look for. They will not be very like the idea of 'religious people' which you have formed from your general reading. They do not draw attention to themselves. You tend to think that you are being kind to them when they are really being kind to you. They love you more than other men do, but they need you less. (We must get over wanting to be needed: in some goodish people, specially women, that is the hardest of all temptations to resist.) They will usually seem to have a lot of time: you will wonder where it comes from. When you have recognised one of them, you will recognise the next one much more easily.[2]

When a Christian becomes distinctive from the masses of godless men, people are drawn to Christ. One of the greatest barriers to bringing men to Christ is the hypocrisy of so-called Christians. In 1923, missionary Theron Rankin met in Canton Commander Boradin, leader of the Russian Communists. Rankin's biographer wrote:

Rankin realized that the Communist hostility was due to a misunderstanding of their Christian objectives and motives in China.
Rankin sought to understand Boradin's point of view. He felt Boradin was hearing ideas he'd never heard before. Rankin wished he could get behind his forehead and see through Boradin's eyes and mind, as Boradin did. Boradin probably identified all Christianity with Greek Catholicism in Russia during the days of the Czars. Rankin tried to picture the concept Boradin had of Christianity from persons he'd met who were called Christians.[3]

Missionaries through the centuries have been hampered by inconsistent Christian living of church members. Nevertheless, the compulsion to make disciples of all men is a Baptist principle motivating Baptist mission enterprise. Evangelism and missions are inseparable concepts in Southern Baptist thought.

Influences Motivating Christian Commitments

No man is isolated from environmental influences. No man is saved in a vacuum. Every human and divine encounter leaves an impression on a man's life.

Three important influences have encouraged public decisions in the experiences of great Baptists: (1) the encouragement of a friend; (2) the impact of Scripture; (3) a previous inclination unheeded.

1. *The encouragement of a friend.* Five Southern Baptist Convention leaders have expressed appreciation for the Christian counsel of a specific person. A. T. Robertson and John A. Broadus were encouraged by pastors.

The first Southern Baptist Convention president, W. B. Johnson, was befriended by a lovely young Christian lady who helped him decide for Christ. The first Southern Baptist Seminary president, Boyce, was encouraged by a close friend who was a new convert. Billy Graham credits a first cousin with a helpful prompting.

2. *The impact of Scripture.* The Holy Spirit's presence has strongly moved through Bible passages to bring men to decision.

Charles Spurgeon was greatly swayed when he heard, "Look unto me, and be ye saved" (Isa. 45:22). George W. Truett responded to Hebrews 10:38: "Now the just live by faith: but if any man draw back, my soul shall have no pleasure in him."

Billy Graham was impressed by Romans 5:8: "But God commendeth his love toward us, in that, while we were yet sinners, Christ died for us." The passage convicting Broadus said: "All that the Father giveth me shall come to me: and him that cometh to me I will in no wise cast out" (John 6:37). Johnson remembered, "I drew them with cords of a man, with bands of love" (Hos. 11:4).

3. *A previous inclination unheeded.* Five of the Baptist leaders studied indicated an earlier temptation to accept Christ that was bypassed. Johnson had been instructed in the Scriptures and "knew by rote the doctrines for which his forefathers had been persecuted, but the spirit had not been quickened by the Holy Spirit."[4]

Richard Fuller had nearly yielded on an occasion four years prior to his actual decision. He wrote: "I felt what I now believe to have been the working of God's Holy Spirit and for a while after, I took pleasure in this service of the Dear Redeemer. I also made a profession of religion. This work, however, if begun was imperfect."[5]

B. H. Carroll's experience was as follows: "I had manifested no

interest, except once or twice mechanically and experimentally. . . .
First one and then another catechized me. . . . I presented myself
for church membership. . . . I had not felt lost, nor did I feel saved.
. . . I merely asked the church to withdraw from me on the grounds
that I was not convicted."[6]

John Sampey was aware of sin during a revival meeting when he
was eleven years old. "I took it for granted that someone would speak
to me privately and help me find the light, but no one spoke a word
to me. . . . I might have found the light much sooner if I had been
guided."[7]

George W. Truett was deeply motivated to become a Christian
from his earliest memories. He wrote about temptations before his
decision at age nineteen:

At the age of six while listening to a country preacher there came
to me a distant and deep awareness of my need for God's forgiving
grace. . . . Very vividly do I recall the longing I had that night for
someone to come to my bed and tell how I could get right with God.
. . . At the age of eleven in a series of meetings . . . I was again very
deeply conscious of my sins in the sight of God and my need for
forgiveness. This consciousness was with me again and again throughout the years that followed until the series of meetings in which I
accepted Christ.[8]

Emotional Responses to the Conversion Experience

The validity of a conversion experience is not governed by the
emotional response at the time of decision. The intensity of emotion
varies greatly. Great Baptist leaders have reported a wide range of
reactions from very slight to actual visions.

J. B. Gambrell reported that he was asked to give his testimony
upon joining the church. He replied, "I haven't any great thing to
tell, I am only a sinner saved by grace."[9]

Billy Graham emphasized that while some conversion experiences
are intensive events, others undergo it as a "casual process." Graham
illustrated with his wife's conversion:

My wife, for example, cannot remember the exact day or hour when she became a Christian, but she is certain that there was such a moment in her life, a moment when she actually crossed the line. Many young people who have grown up in Christian homes and had the benefit of Christian training are unaware of the time when they committed their lives to Christ.[10]

Similarly, J. L. M. Curry, Baptist leader and United States ambassador to Spain, reported:

I have never had any rapturous experience, any overpowering views of my sinfulness or forgiveness, and to this day with humiliation I record that I've never had any special satisfaction in partaking of the Lord's Supper. . . . I've often wished for the experiences that some Christians have but they have been denied me or possibly by unbelief I have denied them to myself.[11]

Slightly more intense was Student secretary Frank Leavell's experience, as he went to the mourner's bench at age eleven:

. . . deeply convicted of my sins and of my lost condition as a boy could possibly be. My mental and spiritual outlook was as black as midnight. Then the preacher explained the plan of salvation. I accepted it outright, in toto. Then I stood up and went forward in confession. There has never been a semblance of doubt about that transaction from that moment until this.[12]

Richard Fuller's experience was even more emotional, accompanied with temporary ecstatic feelings in which elements of nature—trees, leaves, earth and sky—seemed to praise God. He had a loss of appetite in which "for days I could neither eat nor sleep [and] I lived upon the love of God." He states: "I found at last what I sought and was filled with a joy which I can never express, unspeakable and full of glory. Creation seemed full of God."[13]

After Fuller's feelings passed away, he concluded, "They would have rendered me unfit to live in such a world."

The experiences of W. B. Johnson and John Sampey were very similar with accompanying visions. George W. Truett's encounter was closely parallel. Johnson, who made his decision in his twenties, said:

One evening after reading the Scriptures and prayer I retired to bed and on closing my eyes there appeared before me a Form like that of the Lord Jesus, with a countenance expression of distress, indicating that although He had died for my sins, I had not received him as my Saviour. This filled my heart with distress and sorrow. After some time I became more calm and fell asleep. In the morning when I awoke my attention was drawn upward to the right, where I beheld the same form I had seen the night before. But, Oh how changed! Instead of distress in his countenance, joy beamed forth upon the attendants around Him, of whom I seemed to be one. He looked upon me with a benignant smile, and a moral change most happy came over my spirit. I felt as tho' the gates of Heaven were opened before me; and in this happy frame I continued for some weeks.[14]

Johnson continued: "My convictions for sin were not of the distressing, alarming character that marks the exercises of some of God's dear children in their conversion to Him. Mine were of a gentler kind, tho' I trust not the less genuine."[15]

Sampey, a former Convention president and Southern Seminary president, told of his encounter:

I had no peace in my heart. The burden of my sin, I could not shake off, and no one told me what I needed to do to get rid of the burden. I was floundering in the slaught of despair. As I lay on the trundle of the bed on the night of March 3, 1877, I could not go to sleep. We had just said my family prayers and father was reading, and mother was knitting. The younger brother had fallen asleep and I was in distress over my sins. In desperation I lifted my eyes up and began to talk in a whisper to the Saviour. I said to Him, 'Lord, Jesus, I do not know what to do. I have prayed, but I get no relief. . . . I have read the Bible, but my sins are still a burden on my soul. I have listened to preaching, but I can find no help. I do not know what to do except turn it all over to you. And if I am lost I will go down trusting you. Then something happened. It seemed that a great presence filled the room, and said to me almost in audible words, 'My boy, I have been waiting for you to do what you have just done. You can count on me to save you. I will not fail you.' My pillow was wet with tears of joy that Christ Jesus was now my personal Saviour![16]

George W. Truett, Convention and Baptist World Alliance president, had a soliloquy with himself at his conversion:

Last night you made a public profession of religion. Now the neighborhood knows about it or will know about it ere the day is done. What have you to say about your public profession of Christ as your Saviour and master this morning, and I put myself to this test. What if Christ should now visibly come into this room and put to you 'are you willing for me to have my way with your life from this time on? I will not indicate to you what that way is to be. It is enough for you to know that my way is always right and safe and best. May I have your consent, without evasion or reservation to have my way with you now and always?' To such tests I gave my unreserved 'Yes' and a great peace filled my heart.[17]

Southwestern Seminary professor W. T. Conner described a peace that accompanied his experience. He wrote:

A number of people talked to me at what was then known as the 'mourner's bench,' but none of them seemed to give me any very definite help. Finally, my load became unbearable, and not knowing what else to do, I gave up.
The expression 'gave up' expresses my experience better than any other I can think of. When I gave up my burden was removed. However, I did not have any great feeling of ecstatic joy; I did not feel like shouting or anything of that kind. I simply felt that my burden was gone and I hardly knew what had happened . . .
Finally somehow, it came to me that I was saved by putting trust in Christ and not in any particular type of feeling that I had had. When I came to that realization, I knew something of what had taken place. I had no sense of ecstatic joy, but I knew that there had been a change in me. Assurance came as I looked to Christ rather than to my own feelings or to anything connected with my own experience.[18]

These testimonies illustrate that there is no set pattern or reaction that accompanies the experience of personal redemption. God works with each individual in the context of his own experiences. The act of surrender or commitment is the common denominator in each evangelical experience. The emotional impact of that decision may be great or virtually nonexistent. The willful dependence upon God's grace is the only ingredient on man's part other than a repentent life for salvation.

Less Effective Ways to Present Christ

The early Christians were instructed to teach unbelievers all things concerning Christ and make disciples of them. This has remained the Baptist missionary imperative until this day. Christians have used a variety of means to fulfil that commission through the centuries. Jesus' personal overtures to the downcast and troubled represents evangelism at its best. Simon Peter's sermon on the day of Pentecost illustrates the most valid form of mass evangelism.

Not every invitation to follow Jesus has been so noble. Popes and church councils invoked an Inquisition during the twelfth and early thirteenth centuries to compel citizens of Northern Spain, Northern Italy, and Southern France to become Christians. Unbelievers were tortured to the point of death, until they yielded themselves to Christ. Pope Pius V, who was later canonized, resorted to the Inquisition in the late sixteenth century to abuse men into turning to God.

Seen in the perspective of the twentieth century, the Inquisition was clearly an unacceptable and ungodly method of evangelism. It was the ultimate expression of appealing to man's base motives for decision.

Southern Baptist leaders have warned of the contemporary dangers of improper appeals. Throughout history some have responded to Christianity much as a "good luck omen." Soldiers in combat foxholes have turned to God with shallow commitments to be assured of safety. Derelicts at rescue missions and starving Chinese abroad often became "rice Christians." This term indicated that they made superficial decisions in order to find food to eat and a place of shelter.

Mass evangelism has been a valid means of drawing men to Christ for nearly two thousand years. Abuses, however, can be seen in some expressions of revivalism. B. H. Carroll had negative adolescent experiences that made him cautious of revivalism. His biographer reports Carroll's fear of improper appeals to follow Christ:

> He knew that men won by an appeal to low motives were never really won, so he never used that appeal. He knew that the twist of a wrist by which he could carry an audience with him with an appeal to the baser motives, but there is not a case on record from the pulpit or on the platform where he resorted to that method. He knew human nature too well to be deceived into the idea that any permanent good could be done by arousing men's passions and carrying a point by the appeal to the ears of the groundlings. This star he followed everywhere. He followed it as conscientiously when speaking to a street rally on the whiskey question, as when he was speaking to a college group on the idealism of Christ.
>
> He has been criticized for not appealing more to the emotions. It has been said that had he been a better judge of human nature, he would have done so. Of it all, he was too good a judge of human nature not to know that any emotional reaction may be spurious and temporary, if not bottomed on a quickened conscience, and enlightened intellect, and a reasonably deliberate judgment. He purposely refused to do permanent harm by using his gifts to win temporary success for his cause, or temporary applause for himself, through methods resulting from an output, so essentially superficial. . . . Along with the power to stir the superficial emotions and arouse the baser passions of men, he had to get to the conscience. A God-given conscience curbed men, sublimated the God-bestowed power.[19]

Carroll was converted to Christ through the influence of an evangelistic service, so his attitude wasn't a blanket condemnation of all forms of mass appeals. Perhaps, he would have resented pointless appeals for men to come forward if they "want to live better." Such a plea from an evangelist may be intended to stir some indifferent soul to trust in Christ. The method, not the motive, troubled Carroll.

W. O. Carver, Southern Baptist Seminary professor, had a similar spirit of caution. His biography states:

> Carver was not a popular evangelistic preacher, because he saw the superficiality of evangelistic preaching and of the results of the converts.

In eagerness to get people to enter the way of salvation by profession to accept plan of salvation by faith and gain assurance of 'eternal life' conceived of in another world, the conduct of evangelism neglected to urge the importance of a qualitative life, communicated by the Holy Spirit, to begin now and to be tested by ethical living in earthly conditions.[20]

The Variety of Conversion Experiences

The personal experience of redemption is the "heart center" of the Baptist faith. E. Y. Mullins suggested a variety of motivations leading to a personal commitment to Christ. He listed love, obedience, hope, and the desire to do the right thing. Mullins' conclusion about conversion experiences was that "repentance and faith are central and essential in every conversion."

Basically, four settings offer the most fertile atmosphere for commitment to transpire: (1) the special preaching service; (2) the fellowship of small groups; (3) cultivation of personal relationships; (4) personal solitude.

1. *Special preaching service.* Since the day of Pentecost, God has blessed the preaching of his word to bring men unto him. This remains so today. Enlistment of unbelievers to worship services appears less effective today than at the turn of the century.

Prominent Southern Baptists have been converted in this manner. Seminary professor and Baptist statesman John A. Broadus was converted in a protracted meeting in 1843. Over ninety years later the charismatic evangelist, Billy Graham, was converted in a similar revival meeting in 1934.

James Boyce, J. B. Gambrell, E. Y. Mullins, and George W. Truett, all Convention presidents, were saved in revival meetings. The distinguished seminary professor A. T. Robertson made his decision for Christ in a revival meeting. Baptist Student secretary Frank Leavell was led to Christ in a protracted meeting, too. Ironically, Major Penn preached the revival in which E. Y. Mullins was saved, and fifteen years later saw Leavell converted in another revival meeting.

Special worship services today bear a remarkable resemblance to the outdoor preaching settings John Wesley and George Whitfield provided.

Young people have turned to Christ in park services in the Sandhills of Central Nebraska. They've trusted Christ through services in the parking lots in Worchester, Massachusetts. Young military personnel have committed themselves to God in outdoor services within several miles of the Strategic Air Command base in eastern Nebraska.

2. *The fellowship of small groups.* New Testament accounts of the early church make frequent mention of fellowship in homes. The third Southern Baptist president, Richard Fuller, accepted Christ as Savior in a small prayer group in 1831. There has been an increasing enthusiasm in response to this type of Christian witness.

Small groups have had a resurgence of evangelistic effectiveness today. A gathering of friends at North Shore, Massachusetts, believed in God through Jesus Christ and established a church. Conversions were seen on the Las Vegas Strip, where a small group of entertainers met backstage for Bible study. An inner-city Philadelphia home became "holy ground" with three hardened unbelievers accepting Christ after a month of Bible study.

3. *Cultivation of personal relationships.* From the time that Andrew introduced his brother, Peter, to Jesus, this has been vital to evangelism. A majority of commitments to Christ are initiated here. Churches engage in a variety of multiple ministries to cultivate friendships that might enable them to care for the whole man. A commitment may come later. It could occur when the person befriended is alone, or possibly in a public meeting.

Friendships with youth and adults are cultivated in a variety of ways today by Christian people. Park recreation programs with Bible study included have enlisted over twenty-five hundred Catholic children in the past five years in Philadelphia. Record Bible school enrolments have been achieved by Nebraska churches using a similar approach.

Through children's clubs in Omaha, Pittsburgh, Cincinnati, Philadelphia, and elsewhere conversions of children and their parents have resulted.

A telephone counseling service in Northeast Philadelphia success-fully prevented suicides and gave new meaning in life to countless numbers of people. A similar project in Worchester is an effective outreach to drug addicts.

A lending library in Lewiston, Maine, has given the minister an opportunity to lead community merchants to Christ.

4. *Personal solitude.* The first and twentieth presidents of the Southern Baptist Convention had conversion experiences of this type, over seventy-three years apart. In 1804, William B. Johnson was at home in bed and yielded his life to Christ. A similar event occurred in the life of John A. Sampey in 1877. Some fifteen centuries before, in A.D. 387, Augustine of Hippo, the early church father, yielded his life to God in a solitary experience in his garden house. Solitude provides a setting for a multitude of thoughts to be sorted out, and acted upon.

The intention of Christ's Great Commission was that men should make disciples while they were going into their various worlds of activity. While going into the neighborhood, or one's job, or in the home, or any other place, Christians are to make disciples. There are many places where the average Southern Baptist is not likely to go in the course of daily events—the Detroit Negro ghetto, the South Dakota Indian reservation, the affluent New York high-rise apart-ments, the white inner-city slums of Philadelphia, the Sandhill ranch areas of Nebraska. Subsidized missionaries are sent to needful places that are seldom touched with an evangelical Christian witness.

In the final analysis every commitment to Christ is solitary. The cultivation and the pleading are simply influences to lead man to the time of personal commitment. The decision to trust God in Jesus Christ is ultimately an experience in personal redemption.

3 A Passionate Concern for the Church

Christianity has had a dramatic resurgence and impact on the American scene during the 1970's. Today the news media, newspapers and television, vie for dramatic coverage of the youthful Jesus People. Twice during 1971 *Time* featured Jesus on its cover. A hit Broadway musical, loosely based on the life of Jesus, is a sellout at the box office. Hymns, such as "Love Lifted Me," "Jesus Loves the Little Children," and "Amazing Grace" have moved from the arena of the church to the Hit Parade in radio broadcasting.

There was a time in the mid-1960's when radical theologians were saying, "God is dead." A member of the famed Beatles singing group, boasted that they were more popular than Jesus. Ironically, today the Beatles are no more. Jesus' following has reached an unprecedented peak in the twentieth century.

But what of these followers! They are called "Jesus Freaks" by their critics. Generally, they are in their teens. Often the conversion to Christ has been a fantastic transformation from an old life-style of drugs, indiscriminate sexual indulgences, and apathy towards life. Most of the confrontations with Christ are occurring beyond the auspices of the organized church. Thousands of these new Christians express doubts about the need for the institutional church.

Baptists passionately believe in the church! They're convinced it's indispensable! Many are perplexed to explain why God is so mightily at work out in the world, when conversions are rather sparse in their church worship services. Furthermore, the enthusiasm with which these new converts cherish the noninstitutional experimental expressions of faith alarms Baptists. The Christian communes or informal campus Bible study groups are no substitute, churchmen declare.

Mature Christian leaders whose own lives were molded and made vital through the church, question the wisdom of the new breed returning to the more primitive expressions of Christianity. Many Baptists would covet the occasion to show the free-spirit Jesus People the vitality and power of the church. Baptists and the enthusiastic Jesus People share much common ground in their understanding of Christian community.

A Common Understanding of Christian Community

Baptists might well enlist and involve many of these young free-lance Christians with a renewed interpretation of their concept of church. Dynamic explanations of a Baptist church's character and mission would excite masses of youth with the New Testament parallels.

First, Baptists don't view the church primarily as an organization. This speaks to the vibrant Jesus People who love and witness for Christ on the streets without the hindrances of external structures. Some organizational structure is necessary in the church. Baptists, however, see the institution and organizations as only practical and outward expressions of the underlying reality. Baptists view the church as God's new humanity amid an unredeemed humanity.

W. O. Carver illustrated the real role of the church: "The church is the core of God's Kingdom as realized in human history. Local churches are the agencies of that kingdom and of its gospel; they are 'colonies' of the kingdom on earth, located in the midst of the world which is to be won through the gospel."[1]

Baptists agree with the Jesus People that the less complex the machinery of the church, the greater the opportunity to worship God. They realize that some have confused loyalty to church activities with loyalty to Christ. God gives people different gifts—some to teach and some to excel in church visitation. As Finley Edge describes it, not everyone is called to visit and should not be made to feel guilty if he serves with his time elsewhere. Reluctance to equate organizational involvement with worship of God turns many youth from the church. Baptists agree that spiritual matters are always in danger of being swallowed up in the institutional but realistically see that some structure is imperative.

Second, Baptists acknowledge expressions of God's power everywhere, but contend it is focalized most mightily through the church. The Jesus People understand this. They know that an individual who walks alone on the streets can encounter God. The intensity of God's power, however, was devastating amid a hundred thousand young Christians at Explo '72 in Dallas. There's no comparison! But Explo '72 was a one-week experience. Such a group encounter is needed regularly. The church alone is a continual focalizing point for a communal encounter with the might and majesty of the living God.

The current of electricity passes through a telegraph wire. Ultimately, there must be an office instrument which localizes the electrical current. God's power resembles the illustration of the current of electricity. It is the church most of all wherein the power of God is localized. If the church is not receptive, the power of God won't come through anymore than electricity would relate to a faulty telegraph instrument. Fortunately, of all places, the church with her congregation of committed believers is most continually receptive. It is thus through the church that God speaks most powerfully year in and year out.

Third, Baptists aggressively undertake the challenge of mission. The principle task of every Baptist church is bringing men to an experience of God through Jesus Christ. Free-spirit Jesus converts zealously share Christ with others. They undertake to win their friends to the Savior immediately. Peripheral matters, admittedly, sometimes take precedence over evangelism in local churches and disaster results. Congregations become lifeless and sterile.

The second largest number of converts were baptised by Southern Baptists in 1971 of their glorious history. The emphasis on personal evangelism by laymen, and the effectiveness of small groups meeting in homes for Bible study achieved a forceful impact for conversions to Christ.

Fourth, Baptists major on the indispensable quality of Christian growth in a community of believers. The Jesus People begin training converts in Bible study from the moment of conversion. Baptists provide the Christian atmosphere and setting where growth, nurture, or sanctification readily occurs. The mature believers delight in sharing experiences and insights into the faith so the new believer will grow in godliness. E. Y. Mullins was right when he said, "This task of making men righteous through the church is utmost in the purpose of a Baptist church."[2]

The stablity and on-going nature of the church provide security and assurance for new believers. W. O. Carver assessed the multinature of the church: "They are not only emigration centers for heaven, but are also recruiting agencies and training instruments and supervising bodies for the recruits as they become active workers in the gospel."[3]

Fifth, Baptists maintain the equality of all believers in the church. The Jesus People have no priestly system. That's one reason they embrace the nonstructured informal Christian crowds. They are brothers in Christ. Baptists have contended the same thing for three and a half centuries, since their beginnings. The concepts of the priesthood of the believer and the equality of Christian brotherhood are basic to Baptist churches. While some denominations have made a very sharp distinction between the minister and the laity, Baptists have a very vague distinction.

Certainly this principle is sometimes abused. A minister may have an exaggerated sense of his own importance and seek to be more dictatorial than a pope. Influential lay leaders may so skillfully manuever church business matters that democracy becomes a mockery. But the danger is even more apparent in nonstructured settings. A single mature Christian may take a new convert under his wing. One teacher becomes a priest to the babe in Christ. The biblical interpretations of the counselor are imposed upon the would-be disciple. The convert is brainwashed by a Christian guru and the biblical concept of the priesthood of every believer is violated.

In the community of believers known as the Baptist church, new converts find an abundance of concerned friends and experience a diversity of biblical interpretation. Through the Spirit's leadership an individual weighs the variety of scriptural views, and finds his own.

Sixth, Baptists employ the practice of home rule. A group of committed believers in an informal Christian commune seek the Spirit's guidance for the community without outside interference. Baptists have always taught that the New Testament taught the same precept. While Baptists encourage and cooperate with many Christian and humanitarian agencies, they are subject to none in spiritual affairs. No other church or association of churches has authority over a local Baptist congregation. No state convention or denominational agency may exert power over a Baptist church.

No governmental power can dictate to the church in matters of organization, faith, worship, or discipline. Neither will Baptists be dependent upon the state for support or favors. The tax exemption common for all nonprofit institutions is the only governmental benefit Baptists accept. Baptists defended this view when it was revolutionary. The separation was based on the realization that mischief resulted when unspiritual men of questionable motives tampered with spiritual and moral matters.

Former secretary of the Foreign Mission Board, Theron Rankin, said:

The most pronounced belief and practice of Baptists, as I have known them in the South, is the sovereignty of each local church, and the conviction that no Convention has Biblical authority to determine the practices of individual churches. . . . As someone has recently said, 'the Convention cannot be an organization or an agency to tell churches what they can or cannot do.' The churches tell the Convention what it can do.[4]

Baptists feel that these apparent New Testament concepts which are basic to the instruction and practice of their churches are appealing to the honest seeker of a church affiliation. There are, however, professed Christians who avoid any church commitment! This is true of Indians on the Oregon reservations. This is seen among blacks in the inner-city of Philadelphia. This is evidenced among the middle American whites in the Sandhills of Nebraska. This is the case for many students on the California coast. This is true of many Jesus

People.

"Why should I join a church?" they cry in honest inquiry. Baptist respect questions from the sincere seeker. Responses of integrity are in order. Baptists willingly seek to present a convincing case on the relevance of the church, from firsthand vital experiences.

Reasons for Expressing Commitment Through Church Membership

First, the relevance of the church is seen in the purpose and manner of its development. The earliest Christians naturally banded together. They wanted to share what they'd experienced and learned. They coveted the fellowship of other believers. During the persecutions they often disguised their identity as Christians. They recognized each other through codes, such as the fish and the sign of the cross.

The church did not develop overnight. But such a community of believers was inevitable! Christians needed encouragement and council from each other. God's Spirit worked through the church to transform and reconcile individuals. Men were renewed from this activity of God through the community of believers.

Through the church saved men expressed the saving impulse of worship and service in practical ways. Public worship was an outgrowth of the fellowship and joy of gathering with fellow Christians. Service for the glory of God became a consuming passion for these inspired followers of Christ.

The church preserved hymns, truth, Scripture, translations, and salvation. This was a most vital contribution of the Christian church.

Later, more formal elements developed in the life of the church. There was need for officers to carry out different responsibilities. External organization was necessary for charitable giving to widows and the economically disadvantaged. The religious ceremonies of believer's baptism and the Lord's Supper were initiated. These elements in the church's life were adopted one by one as needed, until the vital incorporation resembled the cells of an organism. Each of the ingredients played a vital part in the lives of the community of believers.

The disciples viewed the religious ceremonies as an indispensable reminder of what they were about. John A. Broadus suggested his preference for the word *sacramentum,* as used by the early Roman Christians. This term was a military oath in which the Roman soldier bound himself unconditionally to obey his general. Broadus conceded that unfortunately the word "sacrament" like many other words in Christian history had come to be employed in ways foreign to its original use. The principle remains, however, that these ordinances of baptism and the Lord's Supper involved an oath to God by the believer.

The New Testament provides a threefold significance to believer's baptism: (1) The element employed represents purification. (2) The action performed represents a believer's burial to sin and resurrection to walk in newness of life. (3) Experiencing the ceremony in the name of the triune God involves an oath of allegiance and devotion to God.

Pagans in the early days of Christianity viewed baptism as a mystical cleansing to wash away one's guilt. They considered it a magic bath out of which a new person emerged. With the passing of time these superstitious views became more and more powerful. Finally, theologians incorporated these superstitions as part of the essence of Christianity.

Baptists believe the cup was given by the Lord for his followers to remember his sacrifical death. The ancient pagans heard the words, "This is my body, this is my blood." They felt Christ was mysteriously in the elements. The pagans swallowed the ingredients, believing Christ's divine life literally entered them and assured eternal life. Soon theologians decided that Christ was not only present in the sacrament, but also special blessings resulted from eating his body and drinking his blood. A new priesthood developed. It was equipped with mysterious powers to consecrate the sacraments and to forgive sins. Eventually, it was felt that God's saving power was the outgrowth of Christian worship, rather than in spite of it.

Despite such perversions of the ordinance ceremonies, a remnant of believers preserved the intended meaning of the solemn service. Seen in their proper setting and development, the ordinances like all other elements in the church's life are vital and strategic. They are a visible reminder of what the church is about.

Second, the relevance of the church is vital in one's understanding of his place and purpose in the spectrum of Christian history. "Who are you? What are the things for which you stand?" These are the questions today's scoffers of Christianity are asking. They want to know who a person represents and what he believes. A nonchurchman is somewhat at a disadvantage to provide a carefully structured theological system, and to explain the framework within which he stands. His credibility among those to whom he ministers is related to his historical heritage. Acceptance of his heritage gives him a hearing for the weightier matters of spiritual convictions.

Baptists faced this problem in the mid-nineteenth century. The English Baptist minister and historian, G. H. Orchard became concerned about Baptist origins in 1823. He believed Baptists could be linked to the days of John the Baptist in historical succession, and he set out to prove it.

Orchard felt this would give Baptists a weapon of considerable value in interdenominational conflict with the more cultured churches with noble histories and great status. He wrote a book on his concept that became popular in America in 1855. J. R. Graves, a Tennessee Baptist editor, published Orchard's book. The view gained overwhelming acceptance throughout the South and for nearly three decades flourished without question.

W. H. Whitsitt, professor of church history at Southern Seminary, later made studies of Baptist history in England in the 1880's. His research in primary source materials caused him to conclude that immersion wasn't rediscovered until 1641 by Anabaptists. Whitsitt had the best of intentions. He felt that truth could only be helpful when it was revealed. He published his findings with the assertion that Baptist history couldn't be traced beyond 1641. Since nearly two and a half centuries had passed, Whitsitt hadn't knocked the props out from under Baptist history. The record and achievement of Baptists spoke for itself. A storm of resistance to Whitsitt's historical conclusions followed. Only one of his critics bothered to challenge the professor with historical data. Others responded emotionally to the suggestion that the theory of an unbroken ancestry was unfounded.

Orchard, Graves, and Whitsitt were sincere men with concern for the place of Baptists in the perspective of Christian history. Despite their diverse conclusions, they searched for their origins in good faith. Whitsitt's view is generally upheld among contemporary historians. While Christian sect groups had similar doctrinal resemblances to modern Baptists in the first fifteen centuries, no organic unity has been proven.

Another concerned Baptist, J. B. Gambrell, had a mediating position. Gambrell felt that the ability to trace one's Baptist ancestry to the New Testament immaterial. Gambrell ridiculed Catholic successionist theories. He compared the history of the Roman church to a man who was given his father's gun. First the ramrod broke and was replaced. Then he needed to buy a new stock. Later the barrel bent, and a new one was needed. Finally, he bought another lock to take the place of the old one. He still had his father's gun, but all the parts were new.

Gambrell suggested another parable for Baptist views of successionism. He told of the man who lost a gray horse. He noted some horse tracks and followed them step by step for many miles. When he discovered the horse, it was a black horse. He'd followed the wrong tracks and found the wrong horse. Gambrell likened this to theories of historical succession. He maintained that tracks aren't worth a cent. Since Baptists have the right horse or have remained true to the New Testament, the lineage back to Jerusalem is unnecessary.

Baptist history speaks for itself, even if it can't be traced back two thousand years. Baptist efforts for freedom of worship and separation of church and state are exemplary. Baptist doctrines represent a harmony with New Testament interpretations of Christianity. Baptist mission efforts have brought men to Christ and bettered their lifestyles for over 160 years.

An indelible imprint on the pages of history has been made by Baptists for three and a half centuries. The para-ecclesial agencies, as Finley Edge calls the unstructured Christians, have yet to illustrate for what heritage with which they identify and how their views will be perpetuated.

Third, the relevance of the church is illustrated in the role it is playing in the redemption of the world. The lineage of the Christian church has had unbroken connections with Jesus, regardless of the uncertain claims of various denominations. For nearly two thousand years the church has proclaimed God's redemptive work in Jesus Christ. Evangelistic and mission efforts have been motivated by, equipped from, and sent out through the church. The church has not been incidental to the work of the kingdom, it has been God's primary instrument.

Elton Trueblood has accurately characterized the church, saying: "The church is essential to the Christian, not because it brings him personal advancement or even inspiration, but because, with all its failures, it is an indispensable instrument for the redemption of the world."[5]

When Paul C. Porter was appointed a missionary to the state of Sao Paulo, Brazil, in 1922 there were only eight Baptist churches. He was busy leading men to Christ. He also set about to begin churches. There were five hundred Baptist churches in Sao Paulo state when Porter retired. Had he enthusiastically participated in personal evangelism to the exclusion of beginning churches, the new converts would have wandered aimlessly, and the long-range impact on Brazil for Christ would have been lessened.

Finley Edge underscored the congregation's role, stating: "The church is a group of people called into existence by God for a mission—his mission, and only those who have heard this call to minister and understand and accept it should be members."[6] Edge concedes that not every member will express mission in the same manner. Some will minister through vocation, others in some needy area of society, and another group through local congregation activities. Nevertheless, Trueblood insists, "Membership, then, is an invitation to missionary effort, and for that reason we can rightly be grateful that it exists."[7]

Baptist churches are made up of really Christian people. Therefore, this missionary task is a natural outgrowth of membership commitment. In some denominations this isn't the case. A parent's dedication allows an infant to be baptized into some church memberships. Baptists accept only those persons who have met, loved and decided on their own volition that they will follow Christ. Baptists may make mistakes! Sometimes they receive members too quickly. Often they exclude them too slowly. But at least Baptist churches try to keep their membership clean and Christian. "The fact is that no great historic force in the religious or political life of the race has ever impressed the world profoundly or changed it radically without taking on an institutional form. Christianity is not exempt from the law."[8]

Fourth, the relevance of the church is evident in man's own need for a stable, on-going community in which he may develop in godliness. Man is a social being. Few things in life are really individual matters. People reach their fullest development through social interchange. A person seeking to learn on his own is at a great disadvantage. The student in the classroom is assisted by the stimulation of other students and the teacher.

A person's patriotism is enhanced by enthusiastically shouting with others in public meetings or singing the national anthem in large assemblies. Similarly, there must be a social expression of the Christian experience for it to come to its full strength and richness. Private prayer is imperative. There is, however, an additional thrill when one joins in heart-felt congregational hymns. God often uses the influence of social emotion to bring people to great spiritual experience.

The Spirit of God isn't confined to a vacuum. Human personality includes the simultaneous and parallel growth of individuality and sociality from the beginning. The reality of this principle in spiritual matters made the Christian church inevitable. The church isn't an arbitrary extra. Nor is it a sort of religious club that is optional to join. "It is the crowning religious expression of that sociality which is part of his very constitution. Because it is that, it becomes the temple of the Holy Spirit in larger ways than the individual temple of a single life can offer."[9]

Without the regular contact with other Christians, and the sharing of experiences and convictions, many would see the flames of spiritual experience flicker or die. Some simply let their souls wither from the lack of encouragement. Men often allow themselves to be dulled by the joys, worries and distractions of life. Vital thoughts that once mattered, become meaningless sounds. In the end, without a community of believers, believers lose all feeling and concern for everything in the inner life.

A voluntary assemblage of people claiming to be spiritual but with no outward badge or conditions of membership would soon loose its identity as a church and take its place with other human organizations maintained for moral purposes in a greater or less degree akin to those of the church. . . . Inquirers and searchers after truth would like to enter the circle and environment of the spiritual, for obvious reasons, and with nothing to test or sift, with no external means of determining the real character of the applicant there is no reason to suppose that the church would not lose its character entirely.[10]

There is a blind Christian lady who sells pencils within the shadow of Philadelphia's City Hall. I visited her when I discovered her daughter was a Southern Baptist. She told me her daughter was off in school but that she herself had belonged to a Baptist church. She had attended a Baptist church in South Philadelphia some years before but was asked embarrassing questions about her blindness. She never returned. For fourteen years the only church she had was Billy Graham's radio broadcast. As helpful as his radio broadcast is, Billy Graham would be the first to admit it is no substitute for the church.

I began pastoring in the winter of 1970 in a section of Philadelphia's inner-city that had severely deteriorated from its original nature. The Home Mission Board purchased a church building in which another denomination had disbanded. The new congregation began with a nucleus of sixteen persons, none of whom had ever been Southern Baptists.

Through a diversity of ministries, such as park Bible schools, informal home Bible studies, children's clubs, and a teen coffeehouse, over one hundred persons were converted to Christ that year. Some of the new converts returned to their own churches with new vitality. There were forty-four of these who were baptized into the membership of our inner-city mission church.

Many of the conversions had been quite dramatic! A man who'd served eighteen years in prison for murder accepted Christ. A seventeen-year-old adulterous wife trusted Jesus. A suicidal teen whose addiction to drugs had left him nothing to live for was saved. A thirty-year-old man who had spent half his life in criminal institutions for a series of crimes was won to Christ. An adulterous woman with several children born out of wedlock was converted. A venereal disease-infected teen-age girl who'd determined to squander her life as a drunken divorcee was saved at seventeen. An emotionally unstable woman living in common-law marriage was led to commitment in Christ. Other conversions were equally spectacular evidence of the love and power of God.

Here was the problem! Our newborn Baptist congregation was made up almost entirely of new Christians. Nearly all the other members were elderly adults in retirement who were unable to formulate intensive friendships and be a nurturing community. Our church was hardly a healing community where new converts could be nurtured to Christian maturity. The mission church had fulfilled one of the main functions of her mission by winning the guilty, dejected, and hopeless to Christ. The lack of mature Christians meant, however, that this congregation more closely resembled the informal, para-ecclesial communities than an institutional church. The problems exhibited by this mission church are problems associated with the informal and ad hoc agencies without roots.

As a result of insufficient members on mission many of the new converts fell by the wayside. My four home Bible study groups provided spiritual nourishment to a remnant of the new believers. Pastoral visitation became the opportunity for lengthy informal pastoral counseling to these people in crises. Another subsidized Home Mission worker and two volunteer staff members had similar opportunities for counseling. But it wasn't enough!

The new converts attended worship services at first. But each new convert needed a genuine and regular encouragement from conscientiously concerned Christian friends. Adequate attention as an expression of Christ's love would have immunized them from the traumas of life, which are escalated in an inner-city concrete jungle.

Stable congregations with at least fifty mature Christian adults could have handled the amazing evangelistic output of this mission church. Every church member needs a core of concerned friends with which he can regularly have sharing and Bible study. He needs to know the acceptance of confessing his joys, sorrows, and sins. He needs to experience the impact of a group banding together for prayer. There should be the freedom to express the weight of a problem of alcoholism or marital tension among Christian friends. Each could both receive and give assistance to another.

The church at her best is the ideal source of hope for people who've only known life as outcasts. Separated families can find reunion. The lonely and friendless can encounter genuine unity. Men fired from their employment can experience a community that inspires maintaining a new job. This is what the reconciliation of God through the church is all about. The church alone provides the fullest dosage and composition for one to realize the blessedness of the family of God.

4 A Passionate Concern for Doctrinal Principles

Francis Scott Key was being held in custody by a British ship, when the English fleet bombarded Fort McHenry at Baltimore in 1814. After a day and night of battle, the skies cleared one morning to reveal the American flag still flying over Fort McHenry. Its presence symbolized the failure of the British invasion. That sight prompted Key to write "The Star-Spangled Banner."

A flag may appear to be a rather insignificant badge or only a symbol. No nation, however, could endure without a flag, either in times of war or peace. Loyalty and courage are generated by a flag in peacetime. A nation's military would be practically helpless without a flag. A navy would be at the mercy of bombardments from allies and enemies alike.

Baptists have a flag, which heralds who they are and for what they stand. The Baptist flag is the basic doctrine they have adopted from the vital New Testament teachings. Unfortunately, many who have seen our flag have seen only the backside. From that vantage point they saw a disproportionate emphasis on secondary matters. As a result, the Baptist message has fallen on unresponsive ears. Many observers of Baptist life feel all that Baptists stand for are: (1) an exaggerated sense of concern over a church's communion participants; and (2) an inverted pyramid of organizational structure with the grass roots people at the top, and knowledgeable leaders at the bottom.

As Baptists tread on the threshold of the twenty-first century, the times demand a transfer of emphasis. A fresh analysis of fundamental principles, and careful consideration of how to communicate them are overdue. It is a valid question as to whether or not Baptists have ever with maximum effectiveness set forth all the contents of their message to the world. Many weighty issues lie dormant at the bottom of the Baptist Pandora's Box. They need to be displayed and emphasized. The arena of controversy has featured only a couple of Baptist ideas at the expense of greater things.

Baptists need to reverse the way our flag is facing so the world will see our major distinctives. Then the total spectrum of our faith's content will have a magnetic impact on sincere searchers for biblical truth. Aruthur Rutledge, executive secretary of the Home Mission Board, has projected a vision of the potential impact of Southern Baptists some four decades from now. By the year 2015 the population is expected to have doubled, reaching 410 million. What will be expected from Southern Baptists?

Using present growth trends, Southern Baptists would grow slightly faster in membership than the total religious population. By the year 2015 Southern Baptists should have twenty-four million members, or 9.3 percent of the total membership of all religious bodies. . . .

I anticipate that our denomination will be well established in practically all fifty states . . . with about thirty-five functioning state conventions. It is altogether likely that there will be much closer corporate relationships between Southern Baptists and Negro Baptists than at present. As a body that will be more nation-wide than any other denomination in the country . . . in A.D. 2015 Southern Baptists will be in position to exert a salutary influence upon the national character beyond anything possible previously.[1]

Distinctive Baptist principles will make Rutledge's dream a reality. In the early years of Southern Baptist advance throughout states north of the Mason-Dixon line, our churches were wanting to express uniqueness. With the best of intentions many emerged excessively narrow in their doctrinal precepts. Person-centered ministries have been a more recent expression of Southern Baptist distinction, as incredible thousands of converts in these areas have come to experience Christ and his church. The source of such evangelical ministries are found in the great doctrines of our faith.

What Is Our Baptist Distinctive?

Little of what Baptists believe is unique or strictly their own! Immediately, one is tempted to insist that believer's baptism by immersion is a Baptist distinctive. This is incorrect! Nearly 10 percent of the Christian world practices the baptism of believers by immersion.

E. Y. Mullins once emphasized the biblical concepts Baptists cherished that other Christians had adopted. "Baptists have won their contention on the following points: Baptism by immersion, believer's baptism, and congregational polity. The scholarship of the world is practically a unit in the view that the New Testament teaches just what the Baptists hold to on these points."[2]

All evangelical denominations share much in common with Baptists. Mullins expressed other points of harmony: "On many vital matters of doctrine, such as the atonement, the person of Christ, and others, Baptists are in substantial agreement with the evangelical world in general."[3]

What is our Baptist distinctive, then? Every believer is capable of making decisions in spiritual matters before God. This is the Baptist distinctive! This was virtually unknown some three centuries ago in Baptist beginnings. George W. Truett addressed three hundred French civil and military leaders in 1919. He told them:

Baptists believe in the competency of the individual in all matters pertaining to the soul. We hold that neither priest, nor ecclesiastical hierarchy, nor state, nor magistrate, nor any other human agency has the right to dictate to the individual soul in matters spiritual. We conceive of religion as being a personal, individual, voluntary and spiritual relationship between a man and his Creator and Saviour.[4]

Several implications are contained in this watershed conviction. First, it means that faith in God is person-centered. This rules out infant baptism where a parent is the mediator between God and the child. This prohibits any human system of priesthood wherein another intervenes in someone's relationship to God. It underscores the truth that faith is one's relationship with God, and not intellectual accent to doctrine.

Stewart A. Newman, former Southeastern Baptist Seminary professor, in an address to the Dover Baptist Association in Richmond said: "If it's good doctrine it's a fairly adequate description of the main thing. But doctrine is one full step removed from faith." Newman describes faith as being like the love a young man feels for a girl. When the young man falls in love, he expresses his feelings for her in words. The words aren't the main thing. They are his attempt to describe what his experience is and what he feels. Dcotrine is like the young man's words. The experience that prompts our doctrine is faith in God through Jesus Christ. Doctrine is a description of our experience and convictions about God.

The doctrine of the competency of the individual also means that "church" is not the main thing. Newman emphasized the proper perspective of the church in saying: "It was a sad commentary on religion the day that faith and church became synonymous. Church is one full step removed from the main thing. Church never should have been a noun, only an adjective. Believers were the 'church-kind-of-people' or 'the church-where-faith-is-found.'"

What Holds Baptists Together

John A. Broadus was once visiting with John Hall, a New York Presbyterian pastor. Hall wondered how Baptists maintained such forceful cooperation and vital efficiency. He noted that Baptists are held together by no ecclesiastical bonds, but simply a "rope of sand."

Broadus' reply was that the "rope of sand" that holds Baptists together is the mightiest bond there is. The ingredients in such a "rope of sand" would include biblical concern, mission involvement, and fellowship.

The opening paragraph of the constitution of the Southern Baptist Convention expresses its purpose in providing "a plan for eliciting, combining and directing the energies of the denomination for the propagation of the gospel." Since the Southern Baptist Convention exists only when its messengers are in session, this purpose is implemented through elected boards and commissions in the interim.

Central to the "rope of sand" and Southern Baptist Convention purpose is doctrine. E. Y. Mullins gave a classic summation of Baptist doctrine in 1907, known as "The Axioms of Religion." He itemized our great and elemental principles. He called it a restatement or defense of the Baptist position. The teachings became a new apologetic or explanation of our faith. They are paraphrased as follows:

1. Belief about God—A holy God oversees the universe with love.
2. Belief about man's relationship to God—The individual has direct access to God.
3. Belief about the church—There is an equality or brotherhood within the church.
4. Belief about morality—Man is a free agent before God to act with his own will.
5. Belief about human relationships—Man must love others, as he loves his own life for the Kingdom's sake.
6. Belief about relationships between church and government—A free church should operate in a free nation.

This is the "Baptist Manifesto." It means Baptists insist on: "the spiritual rights of mankind: the competency of the soul in religion under God, the equality of all men in direct dealing with God, the equal rights of believers in the church, the principle of responsibility, as growing out of the freedom of the soul. The axioms of religion lie at the heart of New Testament Christianity.[5]

George W. Truett stressed the implications of this principle when he said:

In our scheme of things there is no room whatsoever for coercion, or the use of physical force, in the realm of religion. . . . I am a Baptist and would rejoice to see men everywhere voluntarily accept the tenents of my faith, because I sincerely believe those tenents to be in harmony with the revealed truths of God; but if by the pressure of the weight of my little finger I could physically coerce every person in the world to become a Baptist, I tell you frankly and truthfully, I would withhold that pressure, even of the weight of my little finger. Religion must be free. The soul must have absolute liberty to believe or not to believe, to worship or not to worship.[6]

What Concepts Grow Out of This Conviction?

In religious matters people have direct and personal responsibility and access to God. This concept is the foundation out of which other doctrines grow. It bears no resemblance to the existentialist philosopy of the secular world's autonomous man which says, "Do your own thing!" God is the guide and the individual is not acting apart from this guidance.

What are some concepts growing out of this foundation?

First is the doctrine of separation of church and state. When a Baptist state convention votes to cut all ties with a denominational college and allow it to become a state school, it is because of this cherished principle. Baptists refuse to receive financial assistance, because they refuse to be dominated, unduly influenced, or controlled by them. Baptists, throughout history, have witnessed compromise and sterility in any church which has been a state church.

Second is justification by faith. Works, finances, and disciples are recognized by Baptists as by-products of the conversion experience. No Baptist would accept the promise that one becomes a Christian through good works, paying of penances, or rigid church disciplines. This marks a distinct difference between Baptists and some other denominations. The sufficiency of faith for salvation asserts man's competency to deal directly with God.

Third is regeneration. This experience accompanies or closely follows justification as a result of the individual's encounter with God. To undergo the regenerate life is to reject the degenerate life. To follow God is to turn from that which is contrary to God. To follow God is more than to parrot Christian ethics through humanitarian efforts. To follow God is to follow the example of Christ, because one's life is rooted to God through Jesus Christ.

Fourth is the demand for a converted church membership. The doctrine of the individual's competency before God has social implications as well. The doctrine embraces social aspects of religion. Infant baptism as admission into a community of believers would be out of the question. The church is a group of individual believers interrelating and organized for mission.

Fifth is the principle of democracy in church life. No hierarchal system or governmental intervention can hinder the personal adherence of a Baptist congregation to the will of God. Neither the president of the convention, nor any denominational dignitary may tamper with the equality of membership. Local church democracy is the logical outgrowth of the individual's competency in religion. Mullins wrote, "Democracy in church government is simply Christ himself animating his own body."[7]

Sixth is the realization of the priesthood of all believers. Just as democracy is the congregational expression of the individual's competency, the individual may relate to God directly. No priest, or pastor, or religious person may intervene in man's relationship with God.

One could be strongly tempted to subscribe to another all his religious needs and problems to deliver to God. Many turn to lifelong friends or total strangers for guidance, as if they were priests, instead of turning to God. But God doesn't do business wholesale—only retail—one by one. This means that the individual may interpret Scripture under the leadership of God's Spirit.

The Flexibility for Baptist Doctrinal Differences

The diversity of Baptist people has been obvious from their beginnings. They've differed over missions, the origin of their denomination, interpretation of the Scriptures, and participation in their ordinances. Three times in the past ten years messengers of the Southern Baptist Convention have fought the "battle of Genesis." Many state conventions have been preoccupied with deliberations on how church ordinances should be observed.

With the dawning of the 1972–73 church year only four state Baptist conventions had doctrinal tests for messengers. Kansas, Northwest (Oregon-Washington), California, and Virginia had the more restrictive constitutions. Virtually, all other states had one basic requirement of messengers—that they come from "cooperating churches who are in sympathy with and support the work of this Convention."

The autonomy of the local church is emphasized in almost every state. This practice resembles that of the Southern Baptist Convention Constitution: "While independent and sovereign in its own sphere, the Convention does not claim and will never attempt to exercise any authority over any other Baptist body, whether church, auxiliary organizations, association, or convention."

Kansas had rejected messengers from any churches that affiliated with the National or World Council of Churches. Its constitution refused to recognize messengers from churches that received Christians from other denominations on statement of faith who had experienced believer's baptism by immersion. The third restriction on messengers was if their churches allowed non-Baptists to observe the Lord's Supper with the membership. The proposed new constitution would put this state convention in line with most of the others.

When Theron Rankin was executive secretary of the Foreign Mission Board, he received an inquiry about different practices by churches in reference to the ordinances. Rankin wrote his opinion:

We do know of a good many churches that will accept immersed members from other denominations, provided these members were immersed as an expression of their spiritual death and resurrection through personal faith in the Lord Jesus Christ as Saviour. I believe these differences are among those things that we shall have to leave to the individual churches to be worked out in terms of the convictions and beliefs of local members.[8]

Rankin elaborated on his reasons for such tolerance in congregational polity, when he wrote:

I have become distinctly concerned about developing trends among Southern Baptists. I am particularly concerned about whether or not the Southern Baptist Convention is to be changed from a Convention of churches into an ecclesiastical body which legislates for churches. . . .

If our state conventions and the Southern Baptist Convention remain as agencies in and through which local churches cooperate in undertakings which the church cannot carry out individually, allowances must be made in such cooperation for individual differences.[9]

Historically, associations of churches rather than state conventions have had the responsiblity of doctrinal refinement. Whenever the associations have rebuked the participation of churches, it has properly been done on a biblical basis. Much of the controversy over ordinances has been based on the tradition of the Landmark Movement, linking Baptist heritage to the first century in an unbroken lineage, rather than on valid scriptural interpretations.

Men with passionate concern for the doctrines of the church have been on both sides of the fence concerning ecclesiastical doctrinal tests. Likewise, godly men have disagreed on the contents of a denominationally sponsored Bible commentary. The question boils down to whether the commentary should take a literal interpretation of Scripture or involve biblical criticism. This passionate issue is discussed more fully in the chapter on authority of the Bible.

Herschel H. Hobbs displayed an earnest zeal for an equitable settlement of the dispute over the commentary at the 1972 Philadelphia Convention. He stressed that the principle of the priesthood of the believer was being threatened. He appealed that Baptists were in danger of becoming a creedal people. Hobbs suggested that "as one studies *The Broadman Bible Commentary* he is free to separate what he sees as chaff from the wheat, and be blessed by the latter."[10]

The Irreducible Minimum for Doctrinal Harmony

William L. Hendricks, professor of Southwestern Seminary, has written of tendencies in all Christian groups to press for uniformity. Hendricks wrote, "Often individual religious leaders or groups have become divisive by insisting that all of their interpretations about every minute point of doctrine must be agreed upon before one is 'really Christian.' "

Hendricks stressed that such differences aren't necessarily bad. He stated that one of the positive justifications of denominations is that the genuine diversity of opinion shows the many facets of the truth of God. Hendricks added: "The demand for uniformity of agreement about numerous doctrines and entire, involved systems of doctrine has proven very divisive in Christian communities."

Some Baptists have more doctrinal views than others. A surplus of convictions doesn't mean they are correct or that the bearer is more devout. Any principles beyond those that are fundamental and basic are peripheral. According to Hendricks, there is a core of truths that is commonly considered the irreducible minimum necessary to be orthodox in the faith. (1) The creating God has acted to redeem the world in Christ. (2) Jesus is the Son of God and the world's Savior. (3) God's fullest revelation was in Christ by whom he has invited man to himself. (4) God's Spirit enables men to experience his redemption. (5) The church has provided the Scriptures and witnesses to them. (6) The ultimate destiny for man is his God who judges and saves.[11]

The Baptist Impact upon the World

The principle of the individual's competency before God was unique to Baptists three hundred years ago. It's not nearly as exclusively Baptist today. Vatican II stressed a person-centered interpretation in religion for the largest church called Christian. Baptists needn't mourn the waning of the doctrine's uniqueness. It should be a source of gratitude that Baptist influence has stretched so far and been so effective.

Many years ago Sir Walter Besant wrote a book entitled *Building the Empire*. Curiously, he omitted Ireland and India from the British Empire. More surprisingly he included Australia, Canada, and the United States. In one sense Besant was correct! He meant that British ideas of liberty had come to fruition in the United States. With a similar analysis, America might be regarded as a Baptist empire. Not only have only Christian groups adopted Baptist doctrinal principles, but also the nation has felt its impact. J. W. Porter once wrote:

While we are not unmindful of the fact that the world is indebted, in large measure, to all Christian people, our present purpose is to consider the Baptist contribution to the spiritual welfare of mankind. First of all, and essential to all, is soul liberty, which from the beginning, has been the trophy of the Baptists. That the right to worship God, according to the dictates of the individual conscience, is a debt that the world owes exclusively to the Baptists, is a closed question in all well-informed circles.[12]

Rufus Weaver wrote a similar appraisal when he stated:

The people of God called Baptists have played an important part in every religious crisis since their emergence in history. They were given the name of Baptist because of their endeavor to maintain a regenerated church membership, and this endeavor led to the emphasizing of the primitive form of baptism. They were the pioneers of religious liberty, and the forerunners of modern democracy. They led the way in carrying the gospel into foreign land. More consistently than any other body of Christian believers, they have emphasized spirituality, and have done more than others to guarantee to the individual his religious rights and consequent responsibilities.[13]

It was E. Y. Mullins' theory that the American government is a projection of the shadow of the New Testament church. The professor drew parallels to the six Baptist axioms of religion with the basic American political axioms. The theological axiom of God being supreme has its counterpart in the state's recognition of a power higher than itself. The religious axiom of direct access to God has a political parallel in the concept that "All men are created free and equal." The ecclesiastical axiom of equal privileges in the church resembles the view that our government is "of the people, for the people, and by the people." The moral axiom of man's free will is similar to the American practice in legal court procedures. The religious-civic axiom stating that a free church should exist in a free state finds that the principle is as much political as religious. The social axiom of loving one's neighbor as oneself has its counterpart in the principle of equality to all and special privileges to none.

Mullins illustrated the Baptist influence with the stalactite and the stalagmite. Baptist principles are like the stalactites which abound from heaven to earth and mankind. The American political society is the stalagmite. Its foundation on earth rises towards the stalactite.

Mullins suggests that when the two connect, "heaven and earth will be joined together and the kingdom of God will have come among men."[14]

Achieving the Dream of a Dynamic Future

The dream that Arthur Rutledge suggested of evangelizing and equipping twenty-four million Southern Baptists just over forty years from now can be a reality. It will depend to a great extent on the willingness of Baptists to be doers of the Word and not hearers only. It will hinge on the passion to respond to the specific needs of a neglected humanity with the tangible expressions of Christ's love. It will necessitate a concerned fellowship in which a basic and essential core of truth is championed by all. It will be the outgrowth of an atmosphere of tolerance and understanding concerning the peripheral areas which can't deal directly with man's salvation.

A meeting of Southern Baptist denominational leadership in Nashville in November, 1968, produced a dramatic confrontation. Before an assembly of several thousand people, someone asked W. A. Criswell, president of the Convention, what actions associations should take with churches practicing open communion and recognizing alien immersion. Criswell's reply was that members of his congregation could never accept such practices. He added that Baptists in Europe had always practiced such polity. He referred to the Baptists of North Carolina, Virginia, and Maryland with whom these views were quite familiar. Finally, Criswell pleaded: "Let's not divide over this! We've got too much to do to divide. We've got the world to win for Jesus Christ."

5) A Passionate Concern for God's Spirit

When some radical theologians pronounced God dead in 1966, many began searching for meaning elsewhere at that time. The founder of San Francisco's Church of Satan claims that "The Satanic Age" began in that year. The Sexual Freedom League emerged then, and hippies began a free sex culture.

Billions of perplexed people around the world dabble in every new fad to find meaning in life. Astrology has had an increasing magnetism in America. Between 1,200 and 1,750 daily newspapers in the United States are said to carry daily horoscopes. The belief in witchcraft has become a popular phenomenon. It has been estimated that in the United States "there are perhaps as many as one hundred thousand witches in all which is about one half the number of clergymen or physicians."[1] At least sixty-eight institutions of higher learning offer courses in witchcraft.

The occult has become a counter-religion. Not only astrology and witchcraft, but palmistry, tarot cards, and spiritualism are aspects of this movement. John Newport has suggested at least two reasons for the growing popularity of the occult: (1) "Many get involved because they are disenchanted with science and technology." (2) "The churches seem to be too rational, cold, impersonal, and remote."[2]

A new movement known as "Neo-Pentecostalism" began to develop within the Christian community in 1960. Charles Trentham, speaking to the Pastor's Conference in 1966, described this experience: "What is new about this kind of pentecostalism is that it is not promoted exclusively by emotionally high-keyed or poorly trained people meeting in store-front churches." The movement has invaded the mainline denominations. Baptists, Catholics, Episcopalians, Presbyterians. Methodists, and thirty-five other denominations have witnessed speaking in tongues by their members.

Writing in *Home Missions,* Watson Mills described the new spiritual awakening:

It's almost as if a 'counter culture' is developing within the ranks of Christendom. The returning the emphasis upon eastern religions, spiritualism, mental telepathy, and mysticism may be parts of the same fabric which smacks of revolution within the ranks of the all too often ordered and institutionalized church. It remains to be seen if the emerging 'counter-culture' is a blessing or a curse. Is God working through this movement to breathe new life into the church or are these experiences the result of the complex and demanding times in which we live? Only time will tell.[3]

Theologians have observed that liberalism is forsaken in wartime. Intellectually oriented Christian believers generally retreat from the abstract and speculative in religion when they fear death. The natural reaction of a man in a crisis is to seek a recovery of the basic and certain truths. This is true in other situations, too.

Southern Baptists adopted statements of faith in 1925 and 1963 which contained theological statements on God and other beliefs. They affirmed: "There is one and only one living and true God. . . . The eternal God reveals himself to us as Father, Son, and Holy Spirit, with distinct personal attributes, but without division of nature, essence, or being."

While this statement remains valid and without dissent, doctrinal statements are waning in popularity. With the United States still involved in the longest war in its history, an experience with God is more desired than words about him. The Vietnam conflict has apparently been one of the circumstances of world events that has driven Baptists back to the basics—a personal encounter with God. Southern Baptist pastors are less concerned with explaining the Trinity and listing the inexhaustible nature of God's attributes. The church is primarily concerned with leading people to God through Jesus Christ.

Southern Baptists will long remember 1972 for three reasons. First, the baptism report released that year indicated that they led more people to Christ than at anytime in their history, except once.

Second, the Philadelphia Convention was assessed as amiable, harmonious, and progressive. This contrasted with the attitudes of some at the 1970 Denver Convention. In Denver the atmosphere of many messengers in the business sessions was void of the "fruits of the Spirit." Instead of love, there was hostility. In place of joy, there was frustration. In lieu of peace, there was fear. Rather than patience, there was intolerance. With a drought of gentleness, there was forcefulness.

Third, there was a far-reaching resurgence of concern for experiencing God firsthand and continuously. The subject of the "Spirit-filled life" had immense popularity in religious retreats, as well as book sales. The peaceful Philadelphia Convention and the impressive evangelistic results were apparently linked to this renewal of faith.

God Speaks in Mysterious Ways

God's Spirit is available to every man. A man's circumstances may hinder God from working within him. God often has to wait until man is ready to receive his bidding. Different methods are required to reach diverse personalities. God has used countless approaches to bring men to himself. God's call to the ministry may take a variety of forms. The common denominator in them all is that God's Spirit is speaking.

Consider six of the many ways that God used to call some of the most effective Southern Baptist leaders into the Christian ministry. God's Spirit employed many means to bring these persons within his will. God speaks through these and other avenues today.

1. *God's Spirit speaks through man's failure and disappointment.*
Former Baptist Student Secretary Frank Leavell was still searching for meaning in life at age twenty-eight. He'd been bored with life insurance, and poor health had caused him to drop out of Harvard Law School. In this time of uncertainty and confusion, God worked through two situations to reveal his will. Leavell became aware of the happiness of Christian service when an older brother went to China

as a medical missionary. Then an opportunity for service opened for him. He was invited to be the secretary for a Baptist Young People's Union in Georgia. He responded to God's Spirit and found a vital purpose in living.

2. *God's Spirit speaks through a person's awareness of great need.*

Billy Graham was a college student in Florida when God's Spirit directed him to his intended calling. Young Graham met and heard many great evangelical leaders who visited his campus. He listened and he heard repeated reminders of the need for a prophet to lead America back to God. This awareness grew on him. He never dreamed he'd be the one God would send. He, like Moses, felt inadequate and unqualified as a speaker. The college president's secretary asked if he didn't feel God was calling him to preach. One night in March, 1938, he finally sensed an unmistakable call while he was alone at the eighteenth green of a golf course. It was there that he fell to his knees and surrendered his life to God as a preacher.

3. *God's Spirit speaks through a gradual and increasing interest within man.*

The former Southern Seminary president E. Y. Mullins had intended to be a lawyer. It was the gradual passion for theology after his conversion that caused him to abandon law and enter the ministry.

Southern Seminary's founder, James Boyce, found that he had an all-consuming interest in the ministry following his commitment to Christ. He felt the call to the ministry following his commitment to Christ. He felt the ministry was the highest place of service, and he had a love of preaching. Boyce, also, realized the shortage of ministers available.

W. O. Carver, missions professor at Southern Seminary, felt he was called to preach from the time he was eight. He looked toward that goal and directed his life to that end. His mother had secretly prayed for his entering the ministry from his birth. He publicly declared his conviction to be a preacher prior to his departure for college.

4. *God's Spirit speaks with the presentation of the gospel.*

Preaching Professor and Baptist statesman, John A. Broadus, had considered the ministry, but didn't feel he was an adequate speaker.

He wanted to practice medicine. During his college years, Broadus heard a challenging sermon on the proper use of one's talents. He knew that any sacrifice on his part would be repaid a hundredfold if one soul was saved through his ministry. He then yielded his life to proclaiming the gospel.

God's Spirit may be working effectively even in times when there is a poor presentation of the gospel. J. B. Gambrell was a military captain when God called him to preach. He was in a worship service in which the minister made a mess of his sermon, inaccurately interpreting the Scripture. Gambrell had a strong and sudden desire to give a proper interpretation of the passage himself. He never escaped that impression.

5. *God's Spirit speaks through the genuine interest of concerned Christians.*

Home Mission Board Secretary Isaac Tichenor had a pastor who believed in him when he was a boy. Tichenor was asked to pray in public as a youth, but initially refused. When the pastor asked him again, he agreed. Later the minister invited him to preach without time for preparation. Tichenor spoke twenty-five minutes on "Search the Scripture." He was licensed to preach by the church, despite his protests. Later, he was given the chance to preach with time for preparation. He preached on "How Long Will You Stay Between Two Opinions." After that sermon he knew for certain he must preach.

Theron Rankin, who became Foreign Mission Board secretary, had hesitations about the ministry as a youth. He knew that he had no finances for college study. His pastor had genuine interest in him and relieved his doubts by helping with financial arrangements. In seclusion and prayer Rankin found the answer that he must preach.

New Testament and Greek professor A. T. Robertson had an inclination towards the ministry after his conversion. His pastor noted the boy's interest and guided him in public prayer. The pastor finally asked Robertson if he didn't feel he was called to preach. The youth admitted such thoughts, and was stirred at the suggestion. He finally responded and was assisted in his education at the pastor's school.

John Sampey, former Southern Seminary president, had encouragement towards the ministry during his youth from a pastor. The minister had been praying for Sampey to become a preacher, and the news
of his pastor's prayers moved him to emotion. The pastor later asked
him if he had been thinking about entering the Christian ministry.
Sampey was informed that the church planned to license him to
preach at the next church conference. He'd always wanted to preach
but had hesitated because of the importance and difficulty of the task.
The prayers of friends and the unanimous action of the church helped
assure him of the decision.

6. *God's Spirit speaks through the church.*

John Sampey heard God's Spirit through the church action, as well
as through his individual friends. In a similar manner, the first Southern Baptist president, W. B. Johnson, heard God's call through the
action of his church. Johnson had a growing feeling of God's call to
the ministry, as a youngster. It was the church who took the initiative.
The congregation met and voted to call Johnson to give public exercise of his gifts. They ordained him for that purpose.

George W. Truett, the famed Dallas pastor, had shown prowess
in public prayer as a young man. He'd also proven effective in publicly
pleading with men to accept Christ as Savior. Members of the church
began asking him if he felt called to preach. The conviction grew
within the church's membership. Within a year, they had a church
conference and called him to be licensed. He protested because of a
desire to practice law. He then requested six months to think it over.
Finally he yielded to the insistence of the church and was licensed
to preach in 1890.

The Encounter with God's Spirit

Every believer in Christ has periodic encounters with God's Spirit.
Some experiences are prolonged! Many are fleeting! Terminology con-
cerning the experience may change from one generation to the next.
The "lordship of Christ" was the emphasis a decade ago. Today the
"Spirit-filled life" is being sought. Both encounters involve commun-
ion with God's Spirit.

Whichever term is used, the prerequisites are the same. First, there is the necessity of repentance. This includes turning away from one's sins with forgiveness. Second, there is the conscious yielding of one's life to God's control.

Through an encounter with God, the submissive Christian may have a variety of reactions. A few will exhibit an inner glow. Some will seek monastic isolation. Others may express emotional fervor with physical or verbal reactions. Though the symptoms may change, a valid and mature encounter with God's Spirit will produce love, joy, peace, patience, gentleness, goodness, faith, meekness, and temperance. An intense emotional experience without the "fruits of the Spirit" is incomplete at best, and possibly invalid.

Faith and repentance are the imperative ingredients to a genuine life in God's Spirit. The emotional characteristics describe one's reaction to the real thing—an encounter with God. They are not "the real thing," nor an adequate substitute for it.

Experiencing God to the Fullest

God is ready to reveal himself to anyone in any circumstances. In certain situations man is more available to God's Spirit. Professor Wayne Oates suggests three disciplines of the Eastern religions that provide an increased consciousness of God or the mystical experience. These disciplines effectively expand one's awareness of the supernatural. When the soil of man's consciousness is fertile, God's Spirit successfully cultivates his soul. Oates lists: (1) fasting; (2) going without sleep; and (3) breathing exercises.

An encounter with God cannot be programmed or manufactured. The working of God's Spirit is best incorporated by the person whose life is eager for godliness. Heightened spiritual experiences are more common to believers who exhibit disciplined expectancy.

Christians with lives tuned in to God's Spirit may have intensive spiritual perception. An individual who suddenly finds forgiveness to relieve a heavy sense of guilt might qualify for a Damascus Road vision.

George W. Truett accidentally killed a friend on a hunting trip. He was uncertain if he'd every preach again. One Saturday night, as he contemplated his future, he prayed and read Scripture. He heard a voice saying, "My times are in thy hands."

During the night he had a dream of Jesus standing beside him, saying: "Be not afraid. You are my man from now on." It occurred three times. After each experience he woke up and told his wife.

The experience of W. B. Johnson's vision at the time of his conversion (told in the chapter on "Personal Redemption") parallels Truett's. One night after reading the Bible and praying, Johnson closed his eyes and saw the form of Christ in distress. Johnson was grieved at first and then fell asleep. The next morning his attention was drawn to the spot where he'd seen the vision. He was immediately at peace when he saw a smile on Christ's lips.

John Sampey was guilty over his sinfulness one night when he was a youth. He couldn't sleep. In desperation he looked up and whispered a prayer to Christ. He committed his life to Christ. Suddenly Christ spoke almost in an audible voice saying that he'd been waiting for that decision. Sampey shed tears of joy at the moment of Christ's compliment.

Different Views on Ways God Works

God's Spirit is meant for guidance and assurance. His presence was never intended for man's displeasure. Discord and tension have resulted in Baptist churches over varying understandings of God and his work in human experience. The central source of friction is the demand by some that all experiences with God conform to a certain pattern. Some prefer a rather sterile stereotype. Others demand that all would speak in tongues. Another group assesses spirituality on the basis of pleasing smiles and frequent phrases, such as "Praise the Lord" or "Amen." These measuring rods of commitment are less reliable and accurate than Paul's guidelines in Galatians 5:22.

Christian ministers frequently recount ways they are led by God's Spirit in pastoral visitation. These are instances of crisis when their presence is desperately needed. The frequency of occurrence is in definite relationship to the sensitivity and receptiveness of the minister to God's Spirit.

I'll never forget the Saturday before Christmas, 1970. I was pastoring an inner-city Philadelphia church. The first home I visited that day was one in which an unemployed new convert had stolen a television set for his daughter's Christmas. His daughter's welfare was all important, and he had no income.

The next home I visited was one in which the father had been laid off work by his factory the previous week. The family with six children had no money for Christmas.

The third home also contained another sad family. The man's company was on strike. His family would have to do without.

It was the saddest Christmas of my life. That day I visited seven homes that would not have a festive Christmas that year.

Every home where I felt God's leadership to visit needed help. I tried to offer hope. A call to area missionary G. W. Bullard brought the hope of available funds for children's presents. The missionary's secretary and a suburban Pennsylvania church collected and delivered over two hundred Christmas presents the next day for the deprived inner-city youth.

The distribution of the presents on Christmas Eve was one of my greatest joys in the ministry. God's Spirit had shown a legitimate need and provided a joyous solution.

Such testimonies abound in the annals of Christian ministries. Other evidences of the leading of God's Spirit deal with assurance one finds in an uncomfortable situation. The gift of the proper words and spirit in a controversial speaking engagement or delicate church conference is God-sent.

By-products of Encounters with God

There are several reactions that are by-products of the personal experience with God. Some are verbal. Others are physical. Glossolalia, or speaking in tongues, has emerged in many churches in recent years. It has been reported by Southern Baptist churches in Pennsylvania, California, New York, Texas, Nebraska, and elsewhere. Some testify that speaking in tongues is an end in itself as an encounter with

God. Others studying the phenomenon, view the indistinguishable verbal sounds as the excited emotional outgrowth of an experience with God.

Professor Watson Mills suggests reasons for the upsurge. "Since it is no longer "acceptable" to talk about God because of certain cultural and technological advances, glossolalia may be one outlet that some are choosing to vent this basic need."[4]

Those speaking in tongues say that the utterances are evidence of a great charismatic revival. I led an interdenominational Bible fellowship group in a Philadelphia home, while serving as missionary. One lady in the group arrogantly boasted that she spoke in tongues. She implied that anyone fully yielded to God would have a similar experience. I heard her boast so often of this special "gift of the Spirit" until it became a little irritating.

Finally, I said: "Since you've experienced the 'least' of the gifts of the Spirit, maybe someday you'll be fortunate enough to have the greatest gift of the Spirit—love."

Enraged, she gazed at me and said in a hostile firmness, "I've always had love, but the tongues have just come recently." Her tone betrayed her words, testimony, and experience.

Glossolalia seldom occurred in the first sixteen centuries of the Christian era. Though rare during the first five centuries, it was almost extinct for the next thousand years of church history. "Only in the twentieth century had glossolalia prospered. . . . The last six decades are, in fact, its prosperous years in which numerous Pentecostal denominations have kept the movement alive."[5]

Similar emotional responses transpired in a 1759 Wesley revival meeting. "Both adults and children fell under the power of the Spirit. They shrieked, swooned, fell to the floor as if dead, babbled senselessly, cried out in praise of God, and so on."[6]

Nearly a half century later in 1803 there were noticable physical symptoms accompanying the spiritual experiences of a Kentucky revival. The meeting

produced several peculiar bodily exercises, such as falling, jerking, rolling, running, dancing, and barking. Perhaps, the most common was the falling exercise which befell all classes. . . . The subject would generally 'with piercing scream, fall like a log on the floor or ground' and appear as dead, sometimes lying thus for hours at a time. . . . The jerking exercise affected different persons in different ways. Frequently one of the limbs only would be affected, sometimes the whole body and often the head alone.[7]

Historians note that such revivalism had a positive influence on the morality of Kentucky. Likewise, the churches saw tangible evidence of the meetings.

"Between 1800 and 1803 more than 10,000 were added to the Baptist churches in Kentucky alone, and there were like increases pretty generally throughout all the western Baptist associations."[8]

Dr. Jack Gray has characterized glossolalia in its proper perspective: "To have a great encounter with God and to come away enamored with the experience rather than with God is sophisticated idolatry. We are not to magnify the gift; we are to magnify the Giver of all the gifts. We are not to go out as an evangel of our gift or our experience, but to be an evangel for God.[9]

The Concerned Response of the Sensitive Believer

How does a believer remain tolerant of an experience he hasn't had and doesn't understand? In the same way that a keenly involved sports fan reacts with unbounded emotion, one having a highly enthusiastic spiritual encounter will have intensive physiological responses.

I was preparing to speak at the Highland Avenue Baptist Church in Brooklyn in the spring of 1972. During the service the pastor asked for testimonies of how people had been blessed by God the preceding week. One attractive girl who neither spoke, nor heard, stood up. She faced the interpreter and communicated of attending a ski retreat for the deaf. She gleamed as she told with sign language of how she had testified to an unbeliever about Christ during the retreat. As she made her meaningful hand gestures, indistinguishable grunting sounds came from her throat. Her excitement over the incident was accompanied by sighs too deep for words.

Though such sounds differ from the speaking in tongues, the principle is the same. Through such sounds, one gives a valid expression of meaningful concern. The sounds may generally be like the childish language of children with indiscernible babbling. The crying and utterances of newborn infants are important.

Tears have long been accepted as a meaningful expression of one's spiritual experience. As long as tongue-speaking is seen in its proper perspective as a by-product of an experience with God, and not as the experience itself, it has a valid purpose. Paul's principle concern was that those with such verbal expressions not disrupt the worship experience of others.

Professor Glen Hinson wisely suggested:

The best advice to those who 'speak in other tongues' would be: Use it for your own edification, but take care lest you make of the gospel a greater offense than need be. The best advice for those who do not have this gift would be: Seek other ways to express the power of the Spirit in the church, but do not suppress and harrass those who claim these gifts, lest you quench the Spirit in your zeal for orderliness and uniformity![10]

Experiencing the Fulness of God

After one has responded to God in faith and repentance, his Spirit becomes an inner reality. The relationship may be nurtured through spiritual disciplines. First, maintain a sense of awe and wonder. When one's spiritual testimony becomes trite to the teller, the wonder is gone. The loss of wonder in an experience uncovers a waning faith.

Second, testify to the workings of God in the present or immediate past. Reminiscing of bygone encounters with God's Spirit is valid. When these experiences come to the neglect of recent testimonies, however, danger is evident. None of the Southern Baptists whose call to the ministry was previously mentioned could have achieved much for God with that single experience. Each of these men came to the wells of God's living water daily for communion with his Spirit.

Oswald Chambers was right, when he wrote, "If you get out of the light, you become a sentimental Christian and live on memories, your testimony has a hard, metallic note. Beware of trying to patch up a present refusal to walk in the light by recalling past experiences when you did walk in the light."[11]

A third discipline is consciously to practice the "fruits of the Spirit." Paul's measuring rod of spirituality included love, joy, peace, patience, gentleness, goodness, faith, meekness, and temperance. He bypassed majoring on the feelings which result from an encounter with God. He stressed the practical and tangible workings of God in human relations.

God's voice comes into man's experience as a gentle wind. The person in perfect communion with God is the most apt to detect and experience it. Those not detecting God's voice miss fellowship with God.

6 A Passionate Concern for Southern Culture

Christian Barnard performed the world's first successful heart transplant in Cape Town, South Africa, in December, 1967. This was a monumental breakthrough in medical achievement. The principle obstacle that Barnard had to overcome was the automatic tendency of the human body to reject any foreign substance entered into it. This principle of the functioning of the human body is paralleled in social cultures, as well.

This is a picture of what happened in the South in the middle of the nineteenth century. Outside forces attempted to dictate a new life-style to the Southern people. A basic threat to the successful agrarian economy was posed by prohibition against slavery. Southerners reasoned that their northern neighbors would have utilized slaves themselves if their environment had been as conductive to agricultural efforts.

The horrible and disastrous effects of the Civil War upon Southern people, their homes, and possessions left the citizens heartbroken. Everything would have to start over. The South needed to be rebuilt. Another unsavory foreign influence was the phenomenon of the Reconstruction Era. All whites who had been either sympathetic to or active in the Civil War were forbidden to vote. Northern carpetbaggers or opportunistic profiteers were selected for public office. Unqualified Negroes were thrust to the forefront in political service. It's not surprising that the Southerners saw their sorrow turn to resentment.

This is the setting out of which the Southern Baptist Convention emerged. Any religious body is inevitably sensitive to the culture in which it is found. Hindsight clearly indicates to twentieth-century

Christians that slavery is a grotesque and inexcusable vice. The Southern Baptist errors and sins of the 1970's, however, will become much more apparent to our children's children.

Any valid appraisal of the passionate concerns of Southern Baptists must take the culture from which it comes into consideration. Southern Baptist teachings and traditions have gradually been altered in the past 128 years, The culture of the South is radically different today from what it was in 1845. Could there be a relationship?

My seminary archaeology professor, Marc Lovelace, illustrated the molding effect of geographical elements. He explained that it wasn't an accident that God chose the large majority of his disciples from Galilee. The diversity of this country with both mountains and plains made for an openness in the attitudes of its inhabitants. Tourists traveled through the land and mingled with the Galileans. The Galileans, therefore, generally had open minds and a willingness to wrestle with new ideas. Ironically, the only non-Galilean Jesus selected was a Judean named Judas. The wilderness and deserts of Judea limited the access of its people to the outside world. Judeans had a narrow base of judgment about world decisions. The people of Judea tended to have closed minds to new ideas.

The Jerusalem church had a cultural problem. Being located in a Jewish culture and originally composed of Hebrew people, Gentiles were treated as second-class Christians. The desire of Hebrew Christians to circumcise all Gentile converts to Christianity was to preserve cultural, as well as religious traditions.

Southern Baptists don't live in a vacuum. They were originally products of the Southern culture. What is the relationship between Southern Baptist adjustments and the coinciding cultural transformations of the South?

The Nineteenth-Century "Southern Strategy"

Contemporary politicians speak often of the "Southern Strategy," which the White House allegedly fosters in order to capture the votes of Southern people. A century ago the "Southern Strategy" was diametrically different. The White House demanded the end of slavery, despite any Southern reaction. The Civil War was the basic strong-arm tactic necessary to accomplish the new law of the land.

The South's affluent economy was crushed! Former Home Mission Board Executive Secretary, Isaac Taylor Tichenor, described the shifting of America's trade center from the Gulf of Mexico to the mouth of the Hudson, as one of the most devastating blows to the South after the war.

Tichenor observed that the configuration of the continents shows that the two great natural trade centers of the world were at the eastern end of the Mediterranean Sea, and on the northern coast of the Gulf of Mexico. The Baptist statesman emphasized that the center in the Eastern Hemisphere had been predominant from the days of the Hittites, Babylonians, Persians, Egyptians, Greeks, and Romans. He stressed that it was England's power and enterprise that disrupted the balance nature had provided and made London the Eastern trade center.

Similarly, in the Western Hemisphere the logical trade center at the mouth of the Mississippi was removed to the Northeastern section of the nation because of the War. Tichenor suggested in 1900 that the disarraying influences will give way to "the pressure of natural conditions and commerce will swing to its normal place, as the needle, when freed from disturbing causes, swings back and points to the pole."[1]

In addition to the crushing effect that the alteration of the trade center had on the South, this area became isolated from the rest of the nation. Historian Samuel Hill states that there was a nineteenth-century phenomenon in which "the South has developed its peculiar way of life along personal, social and religious lines. It has been a region apart, a distinctive subculture within the national culture." Hill elaborated with the contention: "The South on the whole lived as a separate region by choice or by default, and there was no compelling cause for non-Southerners to disturb the South in its regional isolation."[2] This isolationism may have been due in part to the South's sagging economy which prohibited Southern people from the luxury of visiting beyond the Mason-Dixon line.

The "rugged individualist" attitude easily developed in such an atmosphere. Every man's personal problems seemed more urgent than the problems of the South in general. The isolation of rural people in sparsely populated areas from their neighbors contributed to the policy of minding one's own business.

Conditions in the South during and after the Civil War made the growth of social Christianity illogical. Churches in the North had been forced to rethink their Christian social values, because of the depersonalizing effects of industrialization and other forms of urban pressures. Circumstances in the South were totally different with a rural, agricultural environment indicating a less complex life-style.

The "Southern Mood" After the Civil War

A defeated people never function with maximum effectiveness. This was true of the children of Israel following their release from the imprisonment in Egypt. This was borne out in the experience of the Israelites after their return from captivity in Babylon. This was true in the experience of the slaves that were freed as a result of the Civil War. It was experienced again in the plight of the Southern whites that had been severely defeated in the military warfare.

During the days in which Southern Baptists embraced the position of individualistic approach to ethical problems they were responding in part to their circumstances. Twentieth-century liberals justify the separatist attitude of radical American Negroes. Rebellious attitudes and individualistic behavior are condoned by church extremists who point for justification to the repression, persecution, and affliction that these people have endured. Unfortunately, the same theologians would look with disdain at the position of Southern Baptists whose individualistic theology had somewhat similar origin.

Following the Civil War the South was struggling to revive it's agricultural economy. Volumes have been written on the inhumane treatment of Southern whites during the period from 1866–77, known as the Reconstruction Era. White participants and sympathizers of the Confederacy were forbidden by law from voting during this period of time. Only black males and whites who had been neutral during the Civil War were permitted to vote. Northern carpetbaggers or opportunists and blacks were the only elected officials in the South between 1866–77. The fact that a Republican administration had brought these unjust laws to bear upon Southern whites led to the South's allegiance to the Democratic Party which would last for nearly a century.

Baptists in the late nineteenth century were intensely "Southern" in outlook. They supported the Confederacy and opposed "radical Reconstruction." Southerners refused to tolerate any northern influences during this period. The social Christianity that had originated in the North could not, therefore, find acceptance among Southern Baptists. Just as the view of the Baptists in the North was the "northern" view of race relations, in the South "the Baptist view of race was the southern view."[3]

It becomes more obvious why Southern Baptists defended the status quo. Whether it was in politics, social issues, economic concerns, or other areas of interests, Southern Baptists' outlook generally coincided with the prevailing attitudes of Southerners in general.

It seems, therefore, that "to criticize Southern Baptists (in the late nineteenth century) is . . . to censure the South for continuing its agrarian economy and not industrializing."[4] Since the situation after the Civil War in the South was quite simplistic and without the complexity of industrialization, the old-time religion was adequate. The "social gospel" which seemed necessary in the industrial North, would have been quite irrelevant in the deep South at that particular time in history.

Cataclysmic changes in the Northern cities had forced social Christianity upon the Baptists of that area. Industrialization had revolutionary effect upon the people. A Southern historian states: "By the turn of the century, industrialization had reshaped every phase of society in the North. . . . The labor class concentrated around the factory sites and created unprecedented problems of urban existence."[5]

The South slowly changed. Southern Baptists made a gradual transition in their ethical positions. In the late nineteenth century South-

ern Baptists were "common people, poorly educated, and drawn from
the lower and lower-middle classes of rural society. People of such
status accept change slowly."[6]

With the advent of the twentieth century, significant developments
effected the life-style of the Southern people. A Baptist author com-
ments: "Southern Baptists, too, have sensed this transition. They have
dealt with it by modifying the character of ministry as their constitu-
ents have moved from farm to town to city, as churches have expanded severalfold, and as educational levels have risen."[7]

Even in the late nineteenth century when Southern Baptists had
lingered behind Baptists of the North in social involvement, "social
concern was more manifest among Southern religious leaders than
has been generally recognized." Though Southern Baptists had been
generally negative toward organized reform movements, they "called
for the assistance of the government in promoting personal purity
laws."[8] Another Baptist historian states that the point at which Southern Baptists did diverge from prevailing views was "on matters involv-
ing personal religious principles." To criticize Baptists of the South
for reflecting Southern views, necessitates reprimanding Baptists of
the North for being molded to the prevailing Northern influences. It
also demands chastising the Lutherans of Germany and the Catholics
of Austria for failing to stand up against Adolph Hitler during World
War II.

Evolution of Individualistic Ethical Approaches

As a denomination, Southern Baptists have had very little to say
about the evils in society until recent times. However, individual
Christian leaders were on the cutting edge for social reform from the
beginning.

J. B. Gambrell, former president of the Southern Baptist Convention, challenged the oppression of the Negro. His remarks may seem
paternalistic by today's standards, but they were courageous. Before
the turn of the century, Gambrell said:

We have a class of politicians, the remnant of Barbarianism who go up and down the country berating the negro to make prejudice in the minds of ignorant white people; and thus, in a dastardly way to ride down an humble, weak race in order to get in office. They degrade humanity. That humanity Christ dignified when he aligned himself with it. With all of it, whatever color, and died for it. . . . If we hold any part of the negroes down, we will have to stay down with them. If we hold any part of our people down in a ditch, we will have to stand in the ditch with them to do it. A new statesmanship will go for the idea that we are to make the most of every man and woman and child in all the land, knowing that if our people are great, all things else will follow.[9]

John A. Broadus has been called "the foremost leader of our history." Broadus was a champion of the dignity and human rights of every man. On September 9, 1852 Broadus wrote a letter to his wife commending *Uncle Tom's Cabin,* a book many Southerners despised. He penned these words: "I have finished Uncle Tom's Cabin. It is exceedingly well written, having some passages of rarely equaled power, and being altogether, so far as I can judge, a very remarkable book. It contains much that is true, and much that is untrue; will do some good, and a great deal of harm, among the Northerners."[10]

Broadus spoke out against the Ku Klux Klan during the 1860's when it would have been safer to remain silent. Professor H. P. Griffith described this ministry of Broadus at the Cedar Grove Baptist Church,

Just after the war when the Ku Klux were committing great atrocities and terrorizing the upper part of South Carolina, I was with Doctor Broadus at a place where a small party of six or eight young men present. They were all strangers to him and some of them were to me. One of the young men introduced the subject of the Ku Klux and several of them put verbal endorsement on the organization, and expressed their approval of it, as many good men did. Doctor Broadus was silent for some time, but finally he spake and I never heard a more scathing rebuke administered than he gave the young men and the Ku Klux. He grew eloquent over the woes already inflicted by the organization, and spoke with withering power of the criminality of lawlessness and of the just retribution that was sure to come. After we had left, I said, "Doctor, you were pretty hard on those young men." He replied, "Yes, I saw that two or three of them were Ku Klux, and I felt it my duty to reprimand them in strong terms."[11]

There was another instance in which Broadus displayed compassion for the persecuted black minority. After an avalanche of instances in which Negroes were lynched, Broadus wrote an article in the *Louisville Courier-Journal* in 1895. His evaluation about the role of the press, permissive court decisions, and the need for justice has a strangely contemporary right about it.

Everybody can see that lynching grows worse and worse. Such practices are contagious. Public description of one case suggests another, where it might not have been thought of. What in the world will all this lead to? As a permanent and growing practice lynching must be destructive of civilization. Is this statement too strong? Think a moment and see if it would not be so.

The greatest trouble is, people say, that the laws are sometimes inadequate, that punishment provided is not severe enough, and especially the lawyers can manage to have guilty men escape if there is any money in the case. Now there is some ground for this view. There has been a tendency, in recent generations, to tone down the punishment for the highest offenses, and to sympathize with, or pity a mild criminal as rather unfortunate than guilty. . . .

There is a goodly number of intelligent Negroes who really take sound and wholesome views of the situation. If we continue to tolerate lynching we lead these better Negroes to think that we are the enemies of all their race.

Now, then, I appeal to thoughtful men wherever the 'Courier-Journal' is read, will you not come out and condemn this business of lynching? Will you not openly discourage and oppose and stop it? We can stop it. Is not this our duty? Is it not time?

I will not apologize for publishing this respectful appeal. As a minister of religion, I take no part in the manipulations of party politics, . . . But this is in no sense a question of party politics. It is a question of justice, of fundamental rights, or essential civilization, of human welfare.[12]

Broadus' plea for law and order, tempered with justice was ahead of its time. The same passion for law and order would be the cry of politicians and clergymen seventy years after his letter.

The chapter on "Christian Ethics" deals with many of the reasons that Southern Baptists preferred individualistic Christian concern over organized social reform. It was due in part to the spirit of individualism, and the atmosphere of pioneer expansion. Baptists did make some notable organized efforts to assist the Negro people.

Interracial Ministries Baptists Performed

Baptists have always believed the principle "Love thy neighbor as thyself." The difficulty Baptists have had has been in knowing exactly how to implement this basic principle of faith. The two most obvious ways that they engaged from the time of the Civil War were in evangelizing the Negro and in providing literacy training and education for him.

State laws forbade the education of Negroes prior to 1865. Broadus said in 1866 that it was never a necessary part of the institution of slavery to keep slaves in ignorance.

The loss of voting privileges was a bitter experience for the Southern white man. The act of sympathizing or fighting for the Confederacy was grounds for rejection of voting privileges after the War. Since whites could not vote from 1866–77, Baptists were not disposed to support the right of Negroes to vote. When the Federal Government finally restored the right of Southern whites to vote, it motivated a change of heart. The year after the white vote was restored, the Southern Baptist Convention acknowledged the right of all freed men to vote. The 1878 Convention passed this resolution, and the messengers accepted a share of the responsibility of preparing the Negroes for this duty.

Northern abolitionists were reported to have "herded to the polls like cattle" the Negro people during Reconstruction. There was ample evidence that the abolitionists bribed many Negro votes. Abuses such as this led former Southern Baptist president J. B. Gambrell to say, "Negro suffrage was a blunder and a crime."[13] Baptists generally favored the elimination of Negroes from politics at the turn of the century for this reason.

Southern Baptist Seminary professor, Basil Manley, stood apart from the masses with his convictions. He made a dramatic statement in 1889: "The only way then to deal with the black man whom we find in America is to give him his rights, cordially, frankly, fully."[14]

Education was the main right the white man wanted to give the Negro. Some leaders encouraged white leaders to devote their lives to the black people, or at least their spare time. Richard Fuller, third Southern Baptist president, said: "I had been resolved when first called to the ministry to confine my labors wholly to our colored population. I was prevented by the hand of God."[15]

J. B. Gambrell said: "I shall never cease to be thankful that my own first pastorate was a Negro church. And I shall bear record always to their warm heartedness in religion, in their readiness to do a large part because simple hearts love."[16]

While Baptists were enthusiastic about providing educational opportunities for the Negroes, integration wasn't even a consideration. One historian has said: "Segregation of the races in public schools was never a controversial issue among Baptists at any time between 1865–1900. They considered it a necessity."

Cultural Factors in Southern Baptist Practice

The withdrawal of Baptists in the South from the Triennial Convention is often attributed to the friction of the North against South. Samuel Hill suggests in *Baptists: North and South:* "It was not the North-South struggle of the nineteenth century which divided the churches. It was the variation in cultures." Since the cultures influenced the economic structures and social customs of the day, it is a realistic conclusion. The framework of the cultures, the variety of social ills, and the total life-style suggested the impracticality of continued religious solidarity.

In the industrialized urban centers of the North, the more organized practical social ministries in the name of Christ were vital. In the rural South revivalist theology continued to prosper. Hill states,

"These rural people were inclined to religion partly because the values of rural life were more personal and the problems were more individual."

Despite the individualistic spirit of the Southern people, after severing ties with the Triennial Convention, there was a need to solidify for fellowship and common concerns. A pattern of ecclesiastical structure was deliberately constructed in such a way that all agencies, organizations, and programs were linked to the inverted pyramidal structure of the denomination. W. W. Barnes contended, that the "new sort of convention" which met in Augusta in 1845 "was more in accord with the ecclesiology in the South."

Twentieth-Century Ethical Involvement of Southern Baptists

Southern Baptists had significantly altered their attitudes toward responding to the social issues in the new world of the twentieth century. In the days following the Civil War, the church had been almost exclusively engaged in a preaching ministry. As conditions in the South changed, the denomination broadened its visions of involvement. The denomination became committed to the care of orphans and the aged. Southern Baptists sought to promote public morality throughout the Southland. Crusades against alcohol, gambling, and political corruption were undertaken. One evaluation of this transformation read: "In view of the fact that Baptist conventions had been organized for the promotion of rather narrow denominational objectives, the inclusion of these objects in the denomination's program is a significant indication of an increase in social concern."

This was only the beginning. By 1910 Southern Baptists had taken a stand toward the regulation of child labor laws. The Convention's Temperance and Social Service Commission condemned more evils in the 1915 Southern Baptist Convention. These were the despicable sweatshops, the improper labor conditions for women and children, the over-populated tentament housing, and "heartless greed and corporate wealth, and graft in politics." These Conventions had followed the example of the 1908 report to the Convention by a committee on civic righteousness. The special Social Service Commission was strengthened with an increased budget and executive secretary in 1947, to consider ethical concerns. This Commission developed into the Christian Life Commission by 1953. This agency took the lead in drafting a statement "Concerning the Crisis in Our Nation," which was adopted by the 1968 Southern Baptist Convention. This statement showed a dynamic concern among Southern Baptists for the ills in society. One paragraph read:

We will strive to obtain and secure for every person equality of human and legal rights. We will undertake to secure opportunities in matters of citizenship, public services, education, employment, and personal habitation, that every man may achieve the highest potential as a person. We believe that a vigorous Christian response to this national crisis is imperative for an effective witness on our part at home and abroad.

Words will not suffice. The time is come for action.

Over a period of time Baptists have changed! The adjustments appear to be for the better. However, the turmoil of the day has not been without pain for the South or Baptists in particular. Hill relates the cultural transition to the present day tensions within the denomination. "The unrest now disturbing the Southern Baptist Convention . . . springs from one principle source, the appearance of a new culture in the southern region . . . Cosmopolitan currents of thought, a higher level of education, urbanization and industrialization, and the eruption of an irreversible social revolution are creating a new situation."

Any progress worth appraising involves pain. Whether it is the birth of a child or a noble idea, pain is a by-product of it becoming a reality. Despite a healthy diversity of opinion within Southern Baptists, they are having their "finest hour," and the Southland is doing likewise.

7 A Passionate Concern for Christian Ethics

Southern Baptist Response to Personal and Public Immorality

The X-rated movie made its television debut on February 28, 1972. The Columbia Broadcasting Company showed the heavily edited version of "The Damned" for the late Monday night movie. The picture was given an X-rating for its original theatrical release.

In over a century and a quarter of ministry, Southern Baptists have consistently defended a personal, biblical morality. These Baptists have given scathing denouncements to individuals or groups practicing a life-style contradictory to the Bible. No expression of immorality has been overlooked in this process. A key case in point occurred in the winter of 1972 in which Southern Baptists responded to the controversial television movie.

Executive secretaries of the Baptist state conventions had been meeting and brought the matter to the attention of the Executive Committee of the Southern Baptist Convention.

An immediate response came from the Executive Committee. They adopted a resolution and sent it to the CBS network. The resolution expressed "opposition to reported plans by the network to carry such movies on late night television."

The CBS authorities were urged "to exercise moral vision and leadership in promptly reversing their decision to show these highly objectionable films on television."

The resolution went on to declare that "the invasions of America's homes with profanity, vulgarity, adultery, incest, homosexuality, child molestation, nudity, and sadism represent a moral challenge of major proportions."

A quick reply came in a telegram from CBS vice-president John Cowden to Porter Routh, Executive-Secretary of the SBC Executive Committee. The telegram said: "CBS has not—repeat—has not made any announcements that it has purchased a large number of X- and R-rated movies, because CBS has made no such purchase and has no intention of doing so."

This instance was only the most recent in a series of Southern Baptist expressions of concern for public morality. Baptists often noted the failure of groups to observe the sabbath, and responded promptly. They raised objections to the violation of the Lord's Day, as early as 1876 when the Centennial Exposition was held in Philadelphia. The 1891 Southern Baptist Convention even passed a resolution suggesting that the fair management heed the plea of 1,235,765 Baptists in closing its gates on Sunday in respect of God and Christian sentiments. The Sunday opening of the 1893 World's Columbian Exposition in Chicago brought an even greater reaction. Baptists sent a barrage of letters to the fair managers and their congressmen for three years prior to this Exposition. They unanimously urged the closing of the fair on Sundays.

Historically Baptists have attempted to maintain high standards of public morality. Many challenges to the motion picture industries efforts have had previewing objections.

The Southern Baptist Convention meeting of 1926 expressed its "uncompromising disfavor for the salacious, and character-destroying [motion] pictures produced and shown the public."[1] On other occasions Southern Baptists expressed displeasure on a variety of subjects ranging from modesty in dress, dancing, dime novels, and circus performances.

The concern of Baptists for the whole person has prompted opposition to anything that might do harm to a person. Baptist denouncements of football, baseball, boxing, beverage alcohol, and tobacco have all sprung from this conviction.

Since Southern Baptists and other Christian groups consistently opposed every manifestation of immorality, it's legitimate to ask, "Why wasn't the effort successful and how did the present laxity in sexual morality develop?" The accepted moral code of the nineteenth century was the biblical tradition. Sexual intercourse outside of marriage was forbidden. Even violators of this position with no Christian orientation respected these strict viewpoints, whether they obeyed them or not. At least the advocates of biblical morality in the last century were not subject to universal ridicule and disrespect as they are today.

The transition from the biblical principles seems to have begun with the advent of World War I. The deteriorating effects of the war set in and sexual permissiveness became widespread. One historian says, "The main result of the transition in sexual morality has not been a change in particular practices, but a complete reversal of whole social attitudes toward sex."[2] While Southern Baptists still maintain the sanctity and exclusiveness of marriage for the sexual relationship, the secular world holds this view in scorn and contempt. The 1960's ushered in an avalanche of couples living together outside of the marital relationship. Contemporary sociologists have suggested that the trend was made popular by international movie stars who flaunted their immoral life-style before the public and were accepted.

A popular television program in 1971 illustrated what the Southern Baptist attitude would be towards the alarmingly increasing practice of cohabitation outside of marriage.

An episode of "Love, American Style" featured a conversation between a minister and two romantic young people who were reluctant to get married. The boy stated, "We love each other today, now. Who knows if we'll love each other a year from now. If things don't work out, we'll split, and no one gets hurt."

The minister smiling at his wife wisely replied, "I don't know how I'll feel five minutes from now. You're right, no one knows. . . . If things get rough, we can't split when we're married! We're committed to try to make it work because we made a promise. There's almost no chance to keep a promise that was never made."

Southern Baptists have frequently focused on obscenity as the target of their wrath. The 1965 Convention passed a resolution, stating in part:

Whereas we find ourselves in the midst of a moral revolution of unprecedented proportions, and

Whereas the mass media including radio, television, movies, and literature greatly effect our total society . . .

Therefore be it resolved: (1) That this Convention urge all responsible Christian citizens to appeal to newsstand proprietors and sellers of all publications to refuse to sell such literature as appeals to purien interests and . . . (3) That this Convention urge the motion picture industry to reinstate and honor its own code of decency.

A similar resolution was passed by the 1968 Southern Baptist Convention. It stated: "We affirm our resolutions of the 1965 Convention relating to our opposition of obscenity, pornographic and offensive publications and entertainment. . . ."

Baptists have stood for individual human rights and have defended the selective practice of birth control and abortion in recent times. The dangers of the population explosion were the subject of a resolution at the 1967 Convention. A resolution was adopted stating that married couples desiring the use of medically approved methods of birth control take advantage of this prevention of pregnancy.

Abortion was the subject of an approved resolution in the 1971 Convention. The resolution stated: "That we call upon Southern Baptists to work on legislation that will allow the possibility of abortion under such conditions as rape, incest, clear evidence of fetal deformity, and carefully ascertained evidence of the likelihood of damage to the emotional, mental, and physical health of the mother."

A rather startling development occurred during the 1964 Southern Baptist Convention. A Hollywood movie star was elected second vice-president of the Convention. Considering the consistently negative attitude that Baptists have had towards the motion picture industry, it was shocking to many. It was a commendable gesture, however, that the Convention would elect a conscientious Southern Baptist in spite of objection to his vocation. This movie star, Gregory Walcott, even offered a resolution in the 1965 Convention, "calling for a Baptist diplomatic unit in Hollywood." Walcott's hope was that a dialogue could be established between the Christian body and the movie industry that would reverse the direction Hollywood films had been heading. Predictably, the resolution was not adopted. Instead, the previously mentioned resolution on obscenity and mass media presentations, such as movies, was adopted.

Much publicity has been given through the news media to Southern Baptist positions on risque movies, drinking, gambling, and tobacco. Other avenues of Southern Baptist ethical concern are often over-looked.

Southern Baptist Approach to Ethical Involvement

The twentieth-century world is contaminated with evil. These evils are most clearly seen in their depersonalizing effects upon man's creativity and human dignity. Southern Baptists and other concerned Christians have responded to this evil in a variety of ways.

The main reaction to social ills in recent times by most Christian church groups has been frantic movements for reform. These activist churches and individuals within the Christian community have relied chiefly upon nonviolent demonstrations against the evils of war, poverty, racial oppression, and other human injustices. The goal is to change attitudes and circumstances through peaceful means. Despite the quest for nonviolent confrontations, bloodshed and anarchy have often prevailed. These Christian groups feel that the need for change is so urgent that an individualistic approach to social evil is impractical.

Advocates of this position rebel at the suggested solution of changing the lives of men to correct the problem. Roger Shinn, a critic, states: "By this time in history that judgment has surely been proved wrong. We always need better people and changed hearts. But we also need better institutions to implement human generosity, to thwart human evil, and to channel organizational processes that unintentionally hurt, as well as help people."[3]

Evangelist Billy Graham answers such skeptics, saying:

There are those who think always in terms of mass action. The masses, group masses, have obligations, duties, and responsibilities.

They feel that the laws must be enacted that will compel the group
to heed those responsibilities and that this is a major part of the
Christian mission. . . . There is no doubt that the church is in danger
of getting off the main track and getting lost on a siding. We have
been trying to solve every ill of society, as though society were made
up of regenerate men to whom we had an obligation to speak with
Christian advice. . . .

The changing of men is the primary mission of the church. The
only way to change men is to get them converted to Jesus Christ. Then
they will have had the capacity to live up to the Christian command
to "Love thy neighbor."[4]

Generally, Southern Baptists would agree with this method of implementing Christian truth. Graham's key point is that the church's
ethical impact upon a non-Christian society is insignificant. The
Christian faith's message slams with greater force upon the members
of the Christian community.

Those who insist upon the church radically influencing the world's
social injustices tend to be inconsistent. These critics would shy away
from my idea of the church imposing Christian principles of personal
morality upon unregenerate people. Practices of adultery, homosexuality, and disregarding the Lord's Day by unbelievers would tend to
be overlooked by many extremist Christian social reformers.

The Baptist position on ethical responsibility was stated by Mullins
in *The Baptist Faith:* "Christ did not deal directly with human rights,
though no teacher ever did so much to establish them. He dealt with
human duties knowing that this was the point needing emphasis.
Christ cannot be claimed as the special patron of any particular reform movement. His cause absorbs all the truth in each of
them."

While Mullins, Graham, and other Baptist leaders would disavow
activist social involvement, as the principle purpose of the church,
there would be some sympathy towards it. J. B. Weatherspoon, Baptist seminary professor and former Chairman of the Social Service
Commission, sought to put Christian social ministries in their proper
perspective:

To try to save society from its ills is not to deny a final judgment: it is not an effort to build a tower of Babel: it is not an effort to substitute a good America for the kingdom of God. It is no substitute for the Gospel. It is rather our response to the spirit of our Lord, who chose us and set us in the midst of men to be instruments of righteousness and peace.[5]

Several years ago on a late night television talk show, Billy Graham was asked the question, "Does the Christian church have anything to offer the Negro people?" Graham's reply was that the church surely did have significance for the blacks. He cited the fact that Martin Luther King began his civil rights' efforts within the Christian church, and not outside of it. Though King's emphasis and techniques in ministry were radically different from Graham's, the evangelist referred to this as evidence of the church's relevancy to all.

Baptist Concerns for War and Peace

Southern Baptists have generally viewed war as a necessary evil. Throughout their history Baptists have generally hoped and prayed for peace, but vigorously defended instances that they considered to be just wars. President George Washington wrote to the Baptists of Virginia in 1789 that Baptists "throughout America, uniformly and almost unanimously were the firm friends of civil liberty, and the preserving promoters of our glorious revolution."

During the Revolutionary War, Baptists, as well as other Americans, resented the invasion of their privacy by the English. The colonists were forced to feed the British soldiers and provide housing, which was a source of humiliation.

Southerners expected God's blessings for a just victory over the Union Army during the Civil War. Abolutionists from the North had infringed upon the private property, slaves, and freedoms of innumerable people across the South. The Southerners supported the war with vigor and were bewildered by their defeat. They were overwhelmed at explaining why God had allowed them to lose since they felt they had been right. Though most Southerners were unrepentant over their involvement in slavery, they felt that God was giving them a lesson through their humiliating defeat.

Southern Baptists had a position in the first World War that the military issues weren't "primarily personal or political, [but] in essence religious, touching the very foundations of the moral laws, concerned with fundamental human rights and liberties." The Southern Baptist Convention went on record in 1921 resolving that "War is contrary to the spirit and teachings of Jesus Christ, and that it is the greatest obstacle to the progress of Christianity." Another resolution in that same Convention declared war: ". . . fully demonstrated in the times in which we live that nothing but the power of the Gospel in regeneration of individual men in large numbers can ever make the world safe for the highest happiness and most real peace.[6]

Conscientious objectors who would not participate in World War II, because of sincere convictions against killing, were given recognition and sympathy by the 1940 Southern Baptist Convention.

A committee on world peace was appointed by the 1944 Convention, with J. M. Dawson named chairman. This committee was given the responsibility "to express, mobilize, and register, where possible, the sentiments of its five and a half million members in behalf of lasting peace, the democratic world, Christian race relations, equal economic opportunity, and religious liberty."[7]

The world mood had changed significantly thirty years later. As a result of the unpopular Vietnam war, and the large number of soldiers going AWOL, the 1970 Southern Baptist Convention refused to reaffirm the 1940 resolution. However, the 1940 resolution, showing understanding to these pacifists, still stands as the official Southern Baptist Convention position.

Former president of the Baptist General Convention of Texas, Jimmy Allen states: "Far too often in Christian history and in more recent experience these men (objectors) are credited in the public mind of being soft or cowardly. While some may hide cowardice under a cloak of pacificism, the true pacifist is anything but a coward . . . He simply cannot reconcile his Biblical understanding of the demands of Christ with the taking of life."[8]

Thus, Southern Baptist Convention action has not been guilty of behaving as the proverbial ostrich with its head buried in the sand in the midst of the tragedy of human warfare. They have feared and sought to avoid war for at least two reasons.

First, war deteriorates family solidarity. Because of this, Southern Baptists realize, says Scudder in *Crises in Morality,* that "war always challenges moral standards, and it seems that sex delinquency is one of its most familiar accompaniments."

Second, war kills. This is of even more crucial importance. As one Baptist minister expressed it: "Of all the insane and suicidal procedures, can you imagine anything madder than this, that all the nations should pick out their best, use their scientific skills to make certain that they are the best, and then in one mighty holocaust offer ten million of them on the battlefields of one war?"[9]

Southern Baptist Pursuit of Racial Justice

John H. Griffin, author of *Black, Like Me* spoke to a chapel assembly at Eastern Baptist College outside Philadelphia in 1967. He dramatized to the students the experiences that he'd previously related in his book concerning the shock he'd encountered by impersonating a black man in the South during the 1950's. Griffin used a chemical that gave him a black pigmentation. With emotional fervor he described the dilemma of not being allowed to leave a bus to use the restroom facility during a rest stop in a small Southern community. He described the filthy overnight lodgings that were available for Negroes in slum hotels. He related how local black pastors would make arrangements in their parishoner's homes for Negro tourists to find decent accommodations. Then he shocked the students by stating that the communities where he'd had these experiences were predominately composed of white Baptists.

This was a realistic view of many Southern attitudes toward race relations in the 1950's. Fortunately, the Supreme Court decisions have helped change laws and attitudes toward racial justice for the better in the intervening time.

Southern Baptists gradually opened their college doors to Negroes. The first Negroes admitted to any of North Carolina's Baptist colleges was in 1961. Two years later, the largest Baptist university in the world, Baylor, voted to integrate.

The Baptist General Convention of Texas received its first Negro messengers in 1961. A survey revealed that in 1963 there were at least 234 Baptist churches in Texas that had policies of open membership, regardless of race.

Southern Baptists pioneered in cooperative racial endeavors in the 1940's. Those daring pledges of the war-time Conventions will surprise many critics of the denomination.

Weatherspoon became the chairman of the Social Service Commission for Southern Baptists in 1943. That year his Commission gave this courageous report:

No word about Christian social service today that failed to include the problem of race relations would have any right to be spoken. It simply cannot be ignored. Ignored, it grows more acute. Or can it solve itself. . . . And the stage is set by this war for one of two issues, an evaluation of face that will either plunge the world into a more bitter race competition in the future and on a larger scale, or usher in a day of inter-racial co-operation for the common good with an abating race prejudice as between the white and colored races. The race question moves inevitably in one direction or the other. . . . We would be unable to blueprint a final framework. We are not that far along. But we can "seek justice, love mercy, and walk humbly" in the spirit of Jesus Christ. We can take the next step in trying to smother our own prejudices in doing unto others as we would have them do unto us.

The following year the Commission's report under Weatherspoon's chairmanship was no less daring.

Hitler has shown the world the lengths to which race prejudice can go, the havoc it can work, the hate it can create, when untempered by the spirit of Christ and unrestrained by Christian conscience. We cannot follow Hitler. We must find a way of justice that will free both races from fear and open the road for the progress of both in this our common land.

Since the vast majority of the American Negroes lived in the South, Weatherspoon and the Commission charged Southern leaders, both black and white to solve the problem in 1945. These leaders were charged "to take the initiative in setting up goals of adjustment in creating the instruments of just and harmonious relationships."

Weatherspoon made an explosive impact upon the 1946 Southern Baptist Convention with his annual report:

We shall continually strive as individuals to conquer all prejudice and eliminate from our speech terms of contempt and from our conduct actions of ill will. . . . We shall protest against injustices and indignities against Negroes, as we do in cases of people of our own race. . . . We shall be willing for the Negro to enjoy the rights granted to him under the Constitution of the United States, including the right to vote, serve on juries, to receive justice in the courts, to be free from mob violence, to secure a just share of the benefits of the educational and other funds and to receive equal services for equal payment on public carriers and conveniences.

At the 1947 Southern Baptist Convention Dr. Weatherspoon pleaded

That our Convention approve a long range program of education among our own people looking toward racial understanding and Christian attitudes in the solution of race problems and encourage Baptist agencies and institutions to promote such a program . . . That the Convention assign to the Public Relations Committee the task of keeping informed concerning legislation and other governmental actions touching race relations, human rights and citizenship, rights or minority groups; and also of expressing the Baptist principle of democratic freedom and justice in situations that call for their emphasis.[10]

The Supreme Court's historic ruling on Civil Rights in 1953 prompted swift action by Weatherspoon and the Commission. The professor's moving plea to the Convention turned a tide of opposition into "the Christian principles of equal justice and love for all men."[11]

Southern Baptists agreed at that Convention to support the Supreme Court ruling.

The Dilemma of Ethical Decision Making

Southern Baptist fluctuation on ethical issues during their 128 years of existence points out the dilemma of always knowing the truth. Decisions made in one generation by Southern Baptists have often been reversed in the next. Negro voting rights is such an illustration. T. B. Maston, professor at Southwestern Baptist Seminary, helped explain the problem in a book published in 1955.

> We have suggested . . . that some activities are wrong within themselves, but that other activities that may not be wrong as such, become wrong for the Christian because of the attitude of others, because of the environment . . . and because of the purposes for which they are ordinarily used. . . . This suggests that right and wrong may be relative.
> If what is wrong is determined by the attitude of others, one might conclude we have a right to participate in a particular activity in one community, but wrong in another. Such a conclusion would be correct. We need to notice one thing: while that which is right in itself may become wrong . . . an activity that is wrong within itself can never be made right because of the environment in which it may be found or the attitude of people toward it.
> Even when the right or wrong is relative, rather than absolute, there is underneath an absolute principle. For example, one basis for the position that what is right may be wrong is the fact that the Christian should not give primary consideration to what he thinks is right, but to what effect his participation in an activity will have on others and on the cause of Christ.[12]

Maston's book was accepted without question and his point of view was not challenged. However, eleven years later in 1966 Joseph Fletcher wrote a book entitled *Situation Ethics.* He exaggerated to an extreme the legitimate principles that Maston had suggested over a decade before. Fletcher's thesis was that "anything and everything is right or wrong according to the situation." Fletcher asserted that "situational factors are so primary that we may even say 'circumstances alter rules and principles.' "

Baptists immediately found loopholes in Fletcher's theory. A primary criticism of Fletcher is that he disregards the scriptural teachings and the leadership of Christ for a nebulous theory of love being the guideline for action. Fletcher anticipated criticisms and analyzed his shortcomings, saying, "Situation ethics presumes more ability to know the facts and weigh them than most people can muster."

Southern Baptist's most noted Christian psychologist, Professor Wayne Oates, summarizes Fletcher's flaw:

The "new" morality, it seems to me, "edits out" these presuppositions of the levels of maturity in the deciding person. The situation ethicist seems to assume that "every man knows best for him." The end result is that each man is encouraged to do what is right in his own eyes, regardless of his particular level of intelligence, age, capacity of perception and discipline in decision making.[13]

The Christian Life Commission planned a forum in Atlanta in 1969 to pit scholars of Christian truth against both Fletcher and an advocate of the *Playboy* philosophy. Southern Baptist debaters achieved their aim and gave a strong, effective witness to Christian truth in contrast to the contemporary expressions of immorality. Fundamentalist Christian newspapers and radio broadcasters, however, began misstating the purpose and nature of the meeting through their mass media presentations. A wave of protest against the forum arose at the June, 1970, Southern Baptist Convention. A number of sincere, but misguided messengers, caught up in the heat of emotion, sought to have the Christian Life Commission dissolved or severely handicapped with drastic budget cuts.

Few Baptists agreed with the substance of Fletcher's theories. However, Maston's remarks that ethical decisons aren't always clear-cut is obvious to most. The believer often is required to make ethical decisions in areas of gray. These choices are not clearly black or white. Quite often it becomes a matter of selecting the lesser of two evil decisions, rather than selecting between right and wrong.

No sincere Baptist could condone the slavery of the nineteenth century. But the circumstances of the nineteenth century rural America help explain it. Baptists today believe in the right of all adults to vote, but because of the circumstances of Reconstruction, they once fought Negro suffrage.

Baptists believe that murder is a sin. The bombing of innocent women and children at Hiroshima, however, was not a cause of great guilt or regret. Countless thousands of Baptists were in sympathy with the alleged slaying of innocent civilians at My Lai in Vietnam in 1968 by a young army lieutenant. Many find nothing inconsistent between this and the Christian conviction about murder.

Baptists preach that the seventh day is the Lord's and it should be kept holy. The seeming impossibility of ethical consistency is seen in the fact that innumerable Baptists support sabbath abuse by eating at restaurants and purchasing goods from service stations or drugstores. Many of these Christians find no contradictions between their legalistic beliefs and their actions.

There are many areas where Baptists act as if ethics were relative. Should the United States have turned the other cheek after Pearl Harbor was attacked by the Japanese army? The logical answer for most would be no. Baptist moral judgment on this subject was characterized by the seminary professor who said: "Killing another person is wrong, but having one's own family murdered by the enemy is also wrong. Retaliation to protect one's family is often the lesser of the two evils." American Presidents have been accused of having "credibility gaps." This means that they often are less than candid, either for the sake of national security or for their own reelection. Lies from the Presidental level are often excused by well-meaning Baptists, if the national security is at stake. This means that some Baptists feel there is justification for breaking the eighth commandment.

Missionaries on the foreign field come into similar ethical crossroads. When a heathen man on foreign soil with many wives is converted to Christ, the missionaries seldom compel the convert to dispose of all but one wife. To do so would necessitate the castoff wives to go into prostitution or die. Therefore, generally the missionaries permit the first generation convert to keep his multiple wives, but make succeeding family generations follow the proper Christian ethic.

Southwestern Seminary professor, H. C. Brown, clarifies this predicament about ethical decision making, when he says,

I do not have difficulty deciding what is right and what is wrong about murder, rape, slavery, bank robbery, and treason. . . . What about hatred of a neighbor? Lust for his wife, cheating on an income tax return, breaking traffic laws, cheating in school, lying, gossip, stealing time from one's employer, and hatred of people of other races?

Moreover, what about failure to train our children, to help people in need, to support good public officials, failure to vote, to defend the innocent, failure to practice love, mercy, justice, and righteousness.[14]

The bulk of man's ethical decisions will come in the realm of these obvious areas. Brown suggests, however, that men's sins may be divided into categories of personal and impersonal. The ethical problems in interpersonal relationships include marriage, extramarital activities, friendships with those of other races and the opposite sex. The impersonal ethical decisions that are complicated by extenuating circumstances include sexual exploitation, labor disputes, unions, health problems, war, law and order, and business.

Southern Baptists candidly admit with the apostle Paul, "Now I see through a glass darkly." In this admission they seek God's will in every decision. While Southern Baptists may not always properly interpret God's answer, they continue to strive for a greater understanding of God's truth. Once God's will has been discovered, Southern Baptists pray for divine power and the Holy Spirit to help them enact the correct decision.

8 A Passionate Concern for an Exemplary Witness

The prominent Japanese minister, Toyohiko Kagawa, was once asked, "Who is the greatest Christian in the world?" Kagawa gave an unexpected answer. "It is probably some little old lady that no one has ever heard about."

Any attempt to select greatest persons involves the probability of overlooking some unknown saint who is more deservingly qualified. This insight prompted layman Howard Butt to observe: "This sort of evaluation is very limited because we cannot truly see things from God's viewpoint, and I think some human estimations of effectiveness may cause quite a chuckle in heaven."

There is reason to marvel at the significance of certain prophetic voices in the two thousand-year span known as the Christian era. In nearly every generation there has been at least one spokesman above the masses, interpreting the truth of God to his age with courage and clarity.

My mind began to wonder how the leadership of the Southern Baptists would compare with giants like Augustine, Luther, Calvin, Edwards, Wesley, Knox, and Spurgeon.

It seemed an impossible dream to determine the most significant men in the history of Southern Baptists. It was, however, a task worth undertaking.

From the days of the second century, Christian apologetics has been utilized by the Christian community. This is the science of defending Christian truth. It deals with fundamental points of the Christian faith that refute attacks of non-Christian opposition. The apologetics offered a Christian view of God and the world. The apologetics served to increase the sense of unity and purpose within the church, as well as disarming her critics.

There are divisions in the thinking of Southern Baptists. The differences are expressed in positions of the views of inspiration on the Scriptures; the relationship of a spiritual ministry to social concern; the relationship of Southern Baptists to cooperation with other Christian bodies; the Christian viewpoint on the war; and the relationship between the white and black people of our nation.

Southern Baptists have been accused of not being relevant to the twentieth century. This accusation has been valid on occasions within the denomination as it has been at times within every Christian group.

This chapter intends to portray the most outstanding or exemplary men in the Southern Baptist tradition. Here, are Southern Baptists at their best. Here is the Southern Baptist apologetic which offers a common denominator of inspiration to our heritage. Here are some of the men who spoke to their cultures with prophetic voices serving as patterns of excellence for one Christian denomination within the church.

Guidelines for Great Baptist Leadership

What are the ideal qualities for Baptist leadership? What exemplary characteristics are necessary as a standard for denominational greatness? What traits provide a measuring rod of excellence among Southern Baptists of the present and future, as well as the past.

The ingredients included by Paul in the "fruits of the Spirit" are basic. The life-style of love is imperative. All other traits are subordinate. One may, however, possess the "fruits of the Spirit" without having leadership ability.

At least six criteria are essential in assessing the most exemplary Southern Baptist leaders.

1. *He must have exerted a positive leadership in some area of the Convention.*

Baptist history abounds in episodes of negative thought and action. J. R. Graves and J. Frank Norris were two illustrations of this trend in the denomination. They fragmented Baptists into bitter factional camps.

The positive achievements of many have accounted for any greatness Southern Baptists deserve. Negative voices inevitably fail to bring progressive achievement in Baptist life.

Leadership in implementing positive ideals is equally essential in calculating "the most exemplary giants" among our co-laborers. One may stand for every great truth without any effective results. It is the Baptist with conviction leading in the struggle for truth that deserves greatness. The aspiring crusader needs a platform from which to convince others to follow. Some have chosen the floor of the association, state convention, or Southern Baptist Convention to positively affect Baptists. Others have launched their efforts from a place of denominational service.

William B. Johnson showed this characteristic when he took the initiative in formulating the Southern Baptist Convention. Johnson had served as president of the Triennial Convention. He'd observed the painful irreconcilable differences between Baptists in the North and South.

Johnson observed: "A new channel must be created through which the liberality of Southern and Southwestern Baptists shall flow, that its streams may go forth to evangelize the world."[1]

Johnson became the first president of the Southern Baptist Convention, after he'd proven his capacity for leadership and achievement.

Southern Baptist Seminary president John A. Broadus provided evidence of his classic statesmanship at the 1879 and 1891 Conventions. At the first Convention he helped to mediate in a question over the future of the denomination. Broadus' courage and persuasion assured the continuation of the Southern Baptist Convention.

The denomination was in turmoil over the issue of creating a new Sunday School Board in 1891. The atmosphere of the meeting was tense with excitement. A major fight seemed inevitable. Professor J. H. Farmer described the events.

The moment had come. The report had been read. Discussion was in order. There was what all felt to be the lull before the storm. Broadus seized the opportunity, stepped to the front and spoke. Every word throbbed with emotion; it was a brief but passionate appeal for peace. The great throng bowed to his will. Not another word was spoken; the report was adopted in silence. And even as I think of the old veteran sitting there, his head buried in his hands, and his whole frame heaving with emotion which if I mistake not, found relief in sobs.[2]

The leader most positively affected by Broadus' statesmanship was J. M. Frost. He described the same scene.

No one knew how, but all saw it done, and acquiesced in the decision. He did what few men may do once, but perhaps no man would try a second time. He did not move the previous question, for that would have failed, but he accomplished the same result through the sheer power of his influence. He made no speech, besought that others would not speak, and waited to see what would happen—a sublime moment of heroism and faith.[3]

Frost proved his own positive leadership as the founder and first secretary of the new Sunday School Board. He initiated an award's program that bolstered Bible teaching throughout the denomination. There were only 10,400 Sunday Schools with 712,000 members when the program began in 1902. Fourteen years later when Frost died, Southern Baptists had 18,000 schools and 1,700,000 members—an increase of 250 percent.

New Testament and Greek professor A. T. Robertson contributed more than scholarship to Baptists. In 1904 he proposed a Baptist World Congress through an article in a Baptist paper. The Baptist World Alliance owes its origin to this man who wrote forty-five books in his forty-six years as professor at Southern Seminary.

The real giants among Southern Baptists, past and present, maintain such a positive leadership.

2. *He must have had an influence beyond Southern Baptists to the larger body of Christendom.*

The prophetic voices throughout the Christian era have always gone beyond the narrow confines of denominationalism, to the larger Christian community. Dynamic Baptist leadership has an effect beyond the circle of Southern Baptist life. Just as the throwing of a pebble into a stream will cause ripples beyond the point of impact, the great feats of Baptist leaders will impress and affect others.

E. Y. Mullins served with excellence as president of three Baptist bodies—the Southern Baptist Convention, the Baptist World Alliance, and Southern Seminary.

Presbyterian theologian John Gresham Machen evaluated Mullins as a "spokesman . . . for the Baptist church in America, also to the Baptist churches throughout the world, and there are many in other communions also who look to him as their spiritual guide."[4]

John A. Broadus wrote *The Preparation and Delivery of Sermons,* a classic textbook that gave him world-wide acclaim. Charles Spurgeon called him "the greatest of living preachers." In 1889 Broadus became the only Southern Baptist ever to preach the Lyman Beecher Lectures at Yale University.

A glowing appraisal of Broadus' ecumenical influence came from B. H. Carroll.

I repeat, that in my judgment he was the foremost Baptist left in the world when Spurgeon died. . . . In what other great and wise man's character were these elements so manifest: simplicity, humility, piety, purity and integrity? . . . What other Baptist of inflexible denominational principles has so won the heart and respect of other denominations?[5]

James P. Boyce is renown among Baptists, as the founder of Southern Seminary. His Christian influence stretched beyond Baptists during the Civil War. He was elected to the South Carolina Legislature in 1862, where he practiced morality in politics for two terms until the War ended.

B. H. Carroll was known among Christian people of Texas as a standard-bearer of morality. Former Texas governor Pat Neff testified that a sermon by Carroll on the "land question" had prompted him to include a "land plank" in his political platform, thereby affecting an entire state.

Before Isaac Tichenor served as secretary of the Home Mission

Board, he was president of the college that became Auburn University. He observed the disastrous financial plight of all Southerners after the War. During the depressing days of Reconstruction, Tichenor sought to lead the people to realize the wealth of mineral resources available. The Southern people had felt their rebuilding depended on their agricultural resources alone, prior to Tichenor's intervention.

John A. Sampey served for forty-six years as an influence on millions of Christians of many denominations. He was the chairman of the Uniform Lesson Committee of the International Sunday School Association for these forty-six years. Through his participation on that committee he helped produce the lesson outlines used by millions of Christians throughout the world.

3. *He achieved excellence in either administration, ministry, or scholarship.*

The masses of men settle for mediocrity in pursuits of life. A few achieve excellence as persons and in their callings. There is a variety of callings. Some minister with their scholarship by instructing countless pupils in college or seminary instruction. Others utilize their administrative skills to direct Baptist agencies and institutions to higher achievement. Still others minister with pastoral concern to a congregation—excelling in this area.

The achievements of Luther, Wesley, and Knox illustrated the ministry at its best. Baptist personalities have attained a comparable impact on their generations.

The administrative genius of Isaac Tichenor saved the deteriorating Home Mission Board from disaster. A historian records a description of his influence in Baptist business matters.

After fifteen years of successful cooperation with growth and enlargement of its plans and enterprises, the Convention came into years of this period in darkness; Dr. Tichenor was in the enjoyment of his congenial task as President of the college at Auburn, Alabama. But he always loved his Baptist people, and did not now fail to keep in close touch with the things that concerned them. He was always present in their deliberative bodies, lending aid and counsel in the solution of the problems growing out of the changed social and economic conditions that followed the Civil War.[6]

James P. Boyce was founder and first president of Southern Baptist Seminary. His administerating prowess was characterized by J. M. Curry, politician and Baptist statesman.

He was a student, a scholar, a teacher, a financier, a philanthropist, and a parliamentarian; in all these and other branches he was not simply mediocre, but he was remarkable and distinguished, not a follower, not a mere floater on the surface and current of thought and affairs, but a leader, a seer, a thinker, a born ruler.[7]

George W. Truett came to prominence in Baptist life in 1883 when he raised $92,000 in twenty-three months to wipe out Baylor University's indebtedness. He became pastor of First Baptist Church, Dallas, in 1897 and remained there forty-seven years. There were 19,531 additions in this period, and the membership increased from 715 to 7,804 persons. He served, with distinction, as president of the Southern Baptist Convention and the Baptist World Alliance. Truett had a further ministry when he was appointed by President Wilson to tour war-devastated Europe after World War I.

B. H. Carroll was a champion of great Baptist causes. He fought to save the Home Mission Board in the late 1880's when its future was in doubt. At the 1888 Convention at Richmond, "B. H. Carroll saw the necessity of the Home Mission Board . . . at that Convention he delivered an address on 'The necessity of Home Missions in Texas' "[8] That address settled the question.

Carroll's statesmanship helped establish the Sunday School Board at the 1890 Convention. Carroll's defense of the Board greatly influenced the Fort Worth Convention's decision to reestablish the board.

J. B. Gambrell was editor of the *Baptist Standard* and served as executive secretary of the Texas Baptist Consolidate Board for six years. He effectively led Mercer in a quest for $100,000 in endowment gifts before coming to Texas. Upon arriving in Texas he led Baptists in a $212,000 fund raising effort to make Baptist colleges debt-free.

He also was an influential force in the realization of the Sunday School Board.

W. O. Carver represented the best in Baptist mission instruction. He was often referred to as "the best informed man in missions in America or in the world." He dedicated special efforts in providing mission training for Baptist women. The Carver School of Missions at Southern Seminary stands today as a continuing agency for mission instruction, because of his efforts.

4. *He engaged in a ministry in which he exemplified Christian ethical activity.*

The Christian faith is based on thoughts in the mind of God. God translates these thoughts into words in the Bible. God's intention for the Scriptures isn't complete until the Christian translates the words into action. A vital element in the Christian experience is relating moral precepts of the Scripture to business and social decisions.

Former secretary of the Historical Commission, Davis Woolley wrote: Your criterion number 4 uses the phrase, "exemplified Christian ethical activity." Of course this could, according to interpretation rule out every one before the Civil War, if you consider the approval of slavery as contrary to ethical activity.[9]

Slavery certainly appears to conflict with Christian ethics. We make such a judgment, however, in light of the outcome of the Civil War and subsequent events. The issues weren't as clear-cut 125 years ago. Even if the Baptist giants of a century ago erred on the slavery issue, they excelled in other areas of ethical concern.

Some Baptist leaders vigorously fought the influence of beverage alcohol. B. H. Carroll engaged in a fight in McLennon County, Texas, to close saloons in 1885. A senator in his congregation at First Baptist Church, Waco, objected to the pastor's intervention in political matters. The senator said, "If your parsons go into politics, scourge them back by stopping their rations." The following Sunday, Carroll preached from the text, "Is it lawful for you to scourge a man who is a Roman and condemned."[10] Carroll later became the leader of an effort to achieve state-wide prohibition.

J. B. Gambrell was the uncompromising foe of liquor traffic. He was urged to run for governor of Georgia in 1896. He agreed, if the party would declare for state-wide prohibition. It was expected by many that he would be nominated governor without opposition. However, the Constitution required six years of residence by a candidate, and he didn't qualify.

Two instances reported in the chapter about concern for ethical activity illustrate John A. Broadus' ethical concern for the dignity of all men. Broadus expressed intolerance for members of hate groups like the Ku Klux Klan. He spoke out against lynch mobs, when they had increasing popularity.

James P. Boyce took great pains for the welfare of the black man. In 1853 while Boyce was ministering in Columbia, South Carolina, he greatly assisted the Negro people. Through newspaper writings and private pleas, Boyce urged that attention be given to the welfare of the Negro population.

Boyce served as a member of the South Carolina legislature during the Civil War. While in this position, he worked effectively with Christian social concern. The government post allowed him to work for the physical, mental, and spiritual welfare of all Southern people.

Following the Civil War the South was crippled. Dill says: "War had left a cruel desolation in its track. The still more cruel decade of armed reconstruction had repressed the most heroic efforts to rehabilitate the Southland." Isaac Tichenor had served as pastor of First Baptist, Montgomery, Alabama, and First Baptist, Memphis, Tennessee. His ministry was broadened when he accepted the presidency of the college that became Auburn University. Here he aided Southern people in discovering available mineral resources to help the state recover. Later, while Tichenor was secretary of the Home Mission Board he initiated educational programs for Negroes and promoted effective city mission work.

5. *He had the courage to stand for unpopular convictions.*

For a person to champion a popular cause that has a wide following among one's peers requires no courage. Anyone can get on the bandwagon of the crusade that requires no risk of one's securities. For one to declare himself, however, for a cause he believes to be true and risk the assurance of a job or personal relationships portrays a badge of Christian courage.

Seldom does an attack against a Baptist institution or employee involve risk on the part of the leading spokesman. The history of the denomination includes numerous instances of positive leadership which did involve such risk.

John A. Sampey showed such courage when he met with the SBC Executive Committee in 1933. Southwestern Seminary was broke. The Texas seminary president, L. R. Scarborough, was prepared to close down operations and resign.

Sampey, president of the sister seminary in Louisville, volunteered assistance, saying: "I may lose my job for what I am about to say. Southern Seminary has some income from endowments on which we can live. I move that Southern Seminary's apportionment be cut and the difference given to Southwestern."[11]

James P. Boyce risked his reputation and that of Southern Seminary when he determined to make seminary education available for men without college training. Boyce contended: "Whenever Baptists have striven to confine their ministry to men regularly trained in college and seminary, they are still comparatively limited in numbers."[12]

E. Y. Mullins steered the Convention through troubled waters in the mid-1920's. During these times the Convention was stirred up over theories of evolution. During the 1923 Convention he preached a message on "Science and Religion" in which he condemned a resolution against evolution. He maintained that it endangered academic freedom. The views of E. Y. Mullins ultimately were defeated, but his courage for minority positions established his courageous leadership.

J. M. Frost proposed a controversial new Sunday School Board in 1890. The concept resulted in strong opposition from many Southern Baptists who remembered the failure of the first Board in 1873. J. M. Gambrell represented the reluctant voices and met with Frost on a subcommittee to work out the details. Frost described that meeting between the two great men,

We spent a whole day together in my room at the Florence Hotel—he and I alone, and yet I venture to think, hardly alone. . . . At the close of the conference he (Gambrell) proposed to let me write the report and even name the location of the Board, provided he would write the closing paragraph. When the report was written and he added his words, they were accepted, provided he would let me add one sentence. He consented and the task was done so far as the sub-committee was concerned. It was the outcome of an effort by two men believing in each other, differing widely at the start, and in the end thinking themselves together.[13]

6. *He had a continuing legacy of life-changing influence.*

Originally, five guidelines were suggested. This final criteria was suggested in correspondence with Gaines Dobbins, professor of Golden Gate Seminary. He wrote:

Your writing project greatly interests me. I've often said that we Baptists have made a lot of history, but we haven't done much to record it; we've produced our share of great leaders, but we haven't done much to perpetuate their memory.

I like your criteria for evaluation. Permit me to add a sixth, "He left a continuing legacy of life-changing influence."

At one point in the early 1880's the work of the Home Mission Board appeared to be a lost cause. Isaac Tichenor breathed new life into the domestic mission's movement. Tichenor helped implement a systematic plan of mission giving within the denomination in 1884, which led to the present Cooperative Program. He established a church building department that assisted over 1,700 churches built during his ministry. He provided the encouragement and support to build up the Sunday School Board. When Tichenor began as secretary of the Home Board in 1883 there were 78 missionaries. Seventeen years later at his death, there were 346 missionaries under appointment. Tichenor left a life-changing legacy in each of these areas.

B. H. Carroll is best remembered as the founder and first president of Southwestern Baptist Seminary. He began the school in Fort Worth in 1908. "The real truth is that B. H. Carroll had been carrying the

Seminary around in his brain and heart many years."

Ray tells how Carroll's impact on Baptists was characterized by J. M. Dawson:

One of the surest tests of the quality of a book is its power to survive. The test of survival is also an accurate test of the worth of a life. B. H. Carroll's pastoral work abides.

Carroll's biographer, Ray, analyzed his best quality:

But another quality of this big human being that I choose to mention is his passionate self-sacrificial devotion to the struggling and ambitious youth. Throughout the land there are scores, yea hundreds of men who he succored and heartened and helped in the time of youthful discouragement in planting their feet in the path of immeasurable successful lives.

W. B. Johnson led in the formation of three Baptist bodies—the Triennial Convention, the South Carolina Baptist Convention, and the Southern Baptist Convention. He served effectively as president of each. Johnson's concern for education was evidenced in his efforts toward the establishment of Columbian College, Furman University, and Southern Baptist Seminary. He was also known as the "Father of female higher education in South Carolina."

J. M. Frost engineered and guided the Sunday School Board from its new beginning to a place of stability and prosperity. One tribute stated: Dr. Frost gave twenty-five years of his life to building for Southern Baptists an institution, which, measured by the income-making power, was worth many millions of dollars. Thus he enriched the denomination, but himself he did not enrich.[14]

John Broadus' textbook, *The Preparation and Delivery of Sermons,* remains a classic textbook after nearly a century of time has lapsed. He helped maintain the solidarity of the Southern Baptist Convention in the 1879 Convention. He urged the approval of the Sunday School Board in 1890. His life was dedicated to the training of preachers and the success of Southern Seminary. At the time of Broadus' death in 1895, J. B. Hawthorne wrote in the *Western Recorder:* "The death of Dr. John A. Broadus has removed from the earth the greatest American Baptist of this present century. Men like Fuller, Wayland, Robinson and Anderson may have excelled him in some particular quality of gentleness, but none combined so many elements of strength and nobility.

James Boyce initiated seminary instruction within the Southern Baptist Convention. He called a meeting to plan the organization of a new seminary in 1857, which the Convention approved the following year. From 1859 until his death in 1888 Boyce's life was devoted to Southern Seminary. He served as Convention president from 1872 to 1879. The denomination again selected him for the presidency in 1888. Sampey wrote, concerning Boyce, at his death: "One of the noblest leaders of Southern Seminary has fallen. He easily takes a place in the galaxy where shines Furman, Fuller, Manly, Poindexter, Jeter, and Taylor."[15]

A Louisville Jewish rabbi evaluated Boyce:

Had he turned his attention to politics, what a senator he would have made! What a president! If he had been thrown among savages, he could have tamed and civilized them, for he was a born leader of men. . . . Before I came to Louisville, I knew Christianity only in books, and it was through men as Boyce that I learned to know it as a living force. In that man I learned not only to comprehend, but to respect and reverence the spiritual power called Christianity.[16]

E. A. McDowell, former Southern Seminary professor, said: "What George Washington was to the American Revolution and the founding of our country, Boyce was to the beginnings of ministerial education among Southern Baptists.

E. Y. Mullins was Southern Baptist Convention President during the tension-ridden 1920's. He led in an historic formulation of a Baptist Statement of Faith. The Statement remained in effect 38 years without any revision. In 1963 the Statement received slight revisions, but remained basically Mullins' handiwork. Mullins guided Baptists through controversies in which the academic freedom of denominational professors was threatened. Mullins was known as "a thoroughly practical, an exact scholar, a careful researcher, perceptive, master of ideals, a master administrator."[17]

The Most Exemplary Southern Baptists

"Who were the ten men with the greatest impact on Southern Baptists?" The answer to this question reveals the most exemplary Southern Baptist leaders.

The criteria for answering this question are listed in the six characteristics named above. Giants among Southern Baptists who measure up to the guidelines may serve as an inspiration to men at all points on the scale of the theological spectrum. So-called liberals and conservatives can identify with these persons. They aren't the petty personalities who seek to dominate Southern Baptist Convention business sessions with restrictive creedal pronouncements. Nor did any forsake the indispensable Baptist foundations, that would cause the entire structure to crumble.

A survey of fifty contemporary knowledgeable Baptists uncovered distinguished selections. A list of the ten greatest Southern Baptist leaders of the past was expanded to thirteen because of ties in the voting. Each individual chosen made a dynamic contribution in sculpturing the Baptist destiny. Each was at the forefront of Southern Baptist life.

The founders of five Southern Baptist institutions were selected—Southern Seminary, Southwestern Seminary, Southern Baptist Convention, Baptist World Alliance, and Carver School of Missions. Executive secretaries of the Home and Foreign Mission Boards, the foremost Baptist statesman of the nineteenth century, and four Convention presidents were named.

The actual order of preference for the most exemplary Southern Baptist leaders was: (1) George W. Truett; (2) E. Y. Mullins; (3) John A. Broadus; (4) W. O. Carver; (5) A. T. Robertson.

The "ten greatest" list was rounded out with several ties: (6) Theron Rankin; (7) "tie" Isaac Tichenor and J. M. Frost; (9) John A. Sampey; (10) "tie" J. B. Gambrell, W. B. Johnson, James Boyce, and B. H. Carroll.

While many men excel in one or two areas of life, few achieve excellence in every category. The thirteen men named above passed the stiff qualifications for versatile leadership and productive ministries.

They were men touched by God's Spirit to experience personal redemption in Jesus Christ. This conversion prompted each man to have an intensive love and study of the Bible. The Bible provided each man with his doctrinal understanding of the Christian faith. Each man chose to perpetuate the doctrinal truth through church-related channels. Since these men were not living in a vacuum, they enabled the church to influence and be influenced by their Southern cultures. A biblical concern for the problems and needs of their cultures determined their Christian ethical response. Because of their passionate Christian commitments, they became exemplary Christian witnesses.

Baptists Making the Selections

The thirteen men selected "most exemplary" were judged by an elite list of Baptist leaders. Those making evaluations included evangelist Billy Graham; the SBC Executive Secretary, a former president of the Baptist World Alliance; four former SBC presidents; fifteen pastors from six states; five college and seminary presidents; eighteen college and seminary professors; two members of the SBC Historical Commission; three editors of Baptist papers; and the Georgia Baptist Historical Commission.

Truett received votes from 90 percent of those persons making selections. Twelve of the seventeen seminary presidents and professors making evaluations, chose Truett. All of the nine college presidents and professors picked Truett, as did eight of the eleven pastors voting.

Mullins was the second most frequently chosen Southern Baptist with 78 percent of the ballots. Fifteen of the seventeen seminary presidents and professors considered Mullins "most exemplary." Mullins was named by all of the college presidents and professors, and by eight of the eleven pastors.

John A. Broadus received 62 percent of the votes cast, with Carver and Robertson gaining 46 percent and 44 percent respectively.

PERSONS VOTING FOR MOST EXEMPLARY SOUTHERN BAPTISTS
Baptist World Alliance President—T. F. Adams; *Southern Baptist Convention Presidents*—Wayne Dehoney, H. F. Paschall, H. H. Hobbs, Louie D. Newton; *SBC Executive Secretary-Treasurer*—Porter Routh; *SBC Historical Commission*—Davis C. Woolley, Martin Bradley; *Seminary Presidents*—Harold Graves, Duke McCall, S. L. Stealey, Olin T. Binkley; *Seminary Professors*—E. A. McDowell, Dale Moody, George Shriver, John Steely, T. B. Maston, Henlee Barnette, Bill Pinson, Morgan Patterson, Robert L. Baker, Hugh Wamble, Cal Guy, John Newport, Gaines Dobbins; *College Professors*—Pope Duncan, Stewart Newman, Harold Tribble, Kyle Yates, Samuel S. Hill, Wallace Denton, L. D. Johnson; *College Presidents*—Carlyle Campbell, Hoyt Blackwell; *Baptist Editors*—John Hurt, Marse Grant, R. G. Puckett; *Pastors*—Harper Shannon, G. Avery Lee, John Claypool, W. O. Vaught, Robert Seymour, John M. Lewis, Claude Broach, Eugene Owens, Edward Pruden, W. W. Finlator, Carlyle Marney; *Evangelist*—Billy Graham; *Layman*—Howard Butt; and the *Georgia Historical Society.*

Notes

Chapter One

[1] Bernard Anderson, *A Rediscovery of the Bible* (New York: Association Press, 1951), p. 11.

[2] Arnold B. Rhodes, *The Church Faces the Isms* (Nashville: Abingdon Press, 1958), p. 17.

[3] A. H. Strong, *Systematic Theology* (Westwood, N.J.: Fleming H. Revell Co., 1907).

[4] Stewart A. Newman, *W. T. Conner, Theologian of the Southwest* (Nashville: Broadman Press, 1964), p. 101.

[5] William Horden, *A Layman's Guide to Protestant Theology* (New York: Macmillan Company, 1955), p. 68.

[6] C. Penrose St. Amant, *Search,* Spring, 1971, p. 7.

[7] T. B. Maston, *Baptist Standard,* August 24, 1957, p. 4.

[8] E. J. Carnell, *Handbook of Christian Theology* (New York: Meridian Books, 1958), p. 143.

[9] E. C. Routh, *The Life Story of Dr. J. B. Gambrell* (Dallas: Baptist Book Store, 1929), p. 153.

[10] E. Y. Mullins, *The Axioms of Religion* (Philadelphia: Judson Press, 1908).

Chapter Two

[1] Oswald Chambers, *Still Higher for His Highest* (Ft. Washington, Pa.: Christian Literature Crusade, 1970), p. 48.

[2] C. S. Lewis, *Mere Christianity* (New York: Macmillan Company, 1943), p. 172.

[3] J. B. Weatherspoon, *Theron Rankin, Apostle of Advance* (Nashville: Broadman Press, 1958), p. 31.

[4] Hortense Woodson, *Giant in the Land* (Nashville: Broadman Press, 1950), p. 5.

[5] J. H. Cuthbert, *Life of Richard Fuller* (New York: Sheldon & Co., 1879), p. 69.

[6] Jeff D. Ray, *B. H. Carroll* (Nashville: The Sunday School Board of the Southern Baptist Convention, 1927), p. 26.

[7] John R. Sampey, *Memoirs of John R. Sampey* (Nashville: Broadman Press, 1947), p. 6.

[8] Powhaten James, *George W. Truett: a Biography* (Nashville: Broadman Press, 1939), p. 23.

[9] Routh, p. 4.

[10] Billy Graham, *Peace with God* (Garden City, New York: Doubleday & Co., 1953), p. 107.

[11] Edwin Anderson Alderman and Armistead Churchill, *J. L. M. Curry: a Biography* (New York: Macmillan Company, 1911), p. 68.

[12] Claude U. Broach, *Dr. Frank* (Nashville: Broadman Press, 1950), p. 24.

[13] Woodson, p. 9.

[14] *Ibid.*

[15] *Ibid.*, p. 10.

[16] Sampey, p. 6 f.

[17] James, p. 25.

[18] Newman, p. 73.

[19] Ray, p. 73.

[20] W. O. Carver, *Out of His Treasure* (Nashville: Broadman Press, 1956), p. 55.

Chapter Three

[1] Sydnor Stealey, *A Baptist Treasury* (New York: Thomas Crowell & Co., 1958), p. 291.

[2] *Ibid.*, p. 211.

[3] *Ibid.*, p. 291.

[4] Weatherspoon, p. 117.

[5] Elton Trueblood, *The Validity of the Christian Mission* (New York: Harper and Row, 1972), p. 93.

[6] Finley Edge, The Greening of the Church (Waco, Word, Inc., 1971), p. 77 f.

[7] Trueblood, p. 79.

[8] Mullins, p. 248.

[9] Stealey, p. 188.

[10] Mullins, p. 248.

Chapter Four
  [1] Arthur Rutledge, Address, Woman's Missionary Union Convention, Dallas, 1965.
  [2] Mullins, p. 71 f.
  [3] *Ibid.,* p. 53.
  [4] James, p. 148.
  [5] Mullins, p. 53.
  [6] James, p. 148.
  [7] Mullins, p. 53.
  [8] Weatherspoon, p. 118.
  [9] *Ibid.*
  [10] Herschel H. Hobbs, *Baptist Standard,* July 19, 1972, p. 4.
  [11] William Hendricks, *The Baptist Student,* January, 1972, p. 36 f.
  [12] J. W. Porter, *The Baptist Message* (Nashville: The Sunday School Board of the Southern Baptist Convention, 1911), p. 110.
  [13] Rufus Weaver, *The Baptist Message,* p. 103.
  [14] Mullins, p. 274.

Chapter Five
  [1] John P. Newport, *Demons, Demons, Demons* (Nashville: Broadman Press, 1972), p. 45.
  [2] *Ibid.,* p. 19 ff.
  [3] Watson Mills, *Home Missions,* p. 13.
  [4] Ibid., p. 13.
  [5] Frank Stagg, Glen Hinson, Wayne Oates, *Glossolalia* (Nashville: Abingdon Press, 1967), p. 46.
  [6] W. W. Sweet, *The Story of Religion in America* (New York: Harper and Brothers, 1930), p. 230.
  [7] *Ibid.*
  [8] *Ibid.,* p. 231.
  [9] J. W. MacGorman, *Alaska Baptist Messenger,* May, 1972, p. 7 f.
  [10] Stagg, p. 75.
  [11] Oswald Chambers, *My Utmost for His Highest* (Fort Washington, Pa.: Christian Literature Crusade), p. 226.

Chapter Six
  [1] J. S. Dill, *Isaac Taylor Tichenor, the Home Mission Statesman* (Nashville: The Sunday School Board of the Southern Baptist Convention, 1897), p. 124.

2 Samuel Hill and Robert Tolbert, *Baptists: North and South* (Valley Forge: Judson Press, 1964), p. 49.

3 Rufus B. Spain, *At Ease in Zion* (Nashville: Vanderbilt University Press, 1961), p. 126.

4 *Ibid.,* p. 211.

5 K. K. Bailey, *Southern White Protestantism in the Twentieth Century* (New York: Harper and Row, 1964), p. 136.

6 Spain, p. 210.

7 Hill, p. 49.

8 Bailey, p. 213.

9 Routh, p. 120.

10 A. T. Robertson, *The Life and Letters of John A. Broadus* (Philadelphia: American Baptist Publication Society, 1895), p. 45.

11 *Ibid.,* p. 222.

12 *Ibid.,* p. 325 ff.

13 Spain, p. 84.

14 Spain, p. 85.

15 J. H. Cuthbert, *Life of Richard Fuller* (New York: Sheldon and Co., 1879), p. 105.

16 Routh, p. 25.

Chapter Seven

1 Kenneth K. Bailey, *Southern White Protestantism* (New York: Harper and Row, 1964), p. 45.

2 C. W. Scudder, *Crises in Morality* (Nashville: Broadman Press, 1964), p. 5.

3 Roger Shinn, *Tangled World* (New York: Charles Scribner's Sons, 1964), p. 58.

4 Billy Graham, *World Aflame* (New York: Doubleday and Co., Inc., 1965), p. 180 f.

5 Foy Valentine, *Christian Faith in Action* (Nashville: Broadman Press, 1956), p. 8.

6 Bailey, p. 42 ff.

7 Outlook, October, 1962 (Wake Forest: Southeastern Baptist Seminary), p. 22.

8 Foy Valentine, *Peace, Peace* (Waco: Word, Inc., 1967), p. 44.

9 H. E. Fosdick, *Riverside Sermons* (New York: Harper and Brothers, 1958), p. 345.

[10] These and others reports are in the *Southern Baptist Convention Annual* for the designated year.

[11] Bailey, p. 143.

[12] T. B. Maston, *Right or Wrong* (Nashville: Broadman Press, 1955), p. 17.

[13] Wayne Oates, *The Holy Spirit in Five Worlds* (New York: Association Press, 1968), p. 79.

[14] H. C. Brown, Jr., *The Cutting Edge,* Vol. I (Waco: Word, Inc., 1969), Introduction.

Chapter Eight

[1] Hortense Woodson, *Giant in the Land* (Nashville: Broadman Press, 1950), p. 116.

[2] Routh, p. 49.

[3] *Ibid.,* p. 50.

[4] Isla Mae Mullins, *E. Y. Mullins, an Intimate Biography* (Nashville: The Sunday School Board of the Southern Baptist Convention, 1929).

[5] Robertson, p. 444.

[6] Dill, p. 37.

[7] John A. Broadus, *Memoir of James Petigru Boyce* (Nashville: The Sunday School Board of the Southern Baptist Convention, 1927), p. 347.

[8] Ray, p. 98.

[9] Personal correspondence with Davis Woolley.

[10] Ray, pp. 75, 152.

[11] Gaines Dobbins, *Great Teachers Make the Difference* (Nashville: Broadman Press, 1965), p. 44.

[12] Broadus, p. 145.

[13] Routh, p. 50.

[14] P. E. Burroughs, *Fifty Fruitful Years* (Nashville: Broadman Press, 1941), p. 161.

[15] John R. Sampey, *Memoirs of John R. Sampey* (Nashville: Broadman Press, 1947), p. 31.

[16] Broadus, p. 348.

[17] Thesis on E. Y. Mullins on file at Southern Baptist Theological Seminary.